Gerd de Bruyn **Contemporary Architecture in Germany 1970–1996**
50 Buildings

With a preface by Wilfried Wang
and an essay by Gerd Zimmermann

Edited by Inter Nationes, Bonn
in cooperation with the
German Architecture-Museum,
Frankfurt am Main

Birkhäuser Verlag
Berlin · Basel · Boston

Translation from German into English: Timothy Nevill

A CIP catalogue record for this book is available from the Library
of Congress, Washington D.C., USA

Die Deutsche Bibliothek – Cataloging-in-Publication Data
Contemporary architecture in Germany 1970-1996: 50 buildings /
publ. by Inter Nationes, Bonn in cooperation with the German
Architecture-Museum, Frankfurt. Gerd de Bruyn. With a preface by
Wilfried Wang and an essay by Gerd Zimmermann. (Transl. from Ger-
man into Engl.: Timothy Nevill). -
Berlin; Basel; Boston: Birkhäuser 1997
Dt. Ausgabe u.d.T.:
Zeitgenössische Architektur in Deutschland 1970–1996
ISBN 3-7643-5737-1 (Basel ...)
ISBN 0-8176-5737-1 (Boston)

© 1997 Inter Nationes,
Kennedy-Allee 91–103, D-53175 Bonn, Germany and
Birkhäuser – Verlag für Architektur,
P.O.Box 133, CH-4010 Basel, Switzerland

This book is also available in a German language edition.
(ISBN 3-7643-5716-9)

Printed on acid-free paper produced from chlorine-free pulp. TCF∞
Editor: Jan Thorn-Prikker
© Cover and Book Design: Heinz Bähr, Cologne
Lithography: Siering GmbH, Bonn
Production: Bonner Universitätsbuchdruckerei
Printed in Germany

ISBN 3-7643-5737-1
ISBN 0-8176-5737-1

9 8 7 6 5 4 3 2 1

Contents

Preface

● Contrary to the expectations of many visitors to Germany, architecture in this country demonstrates astonishing diversity. Of course, here as elsewhere, one finds many characterless buildings produced by commercially-oriented "architecture factories", which were commissioned by equally widespread and business-minded big companies – but there also exists a surprising architectural richness, which is largely the outcome of the diversity of Germany's federal structure. Chambers of architecture in the individual Federal *Laender* thus encourage the further development of existing local traditions. Even more impressive, however, is the work of foreign architects who have contributed a great deal towards new architecture in Germany.

Internationally celebrated architects – such as Alvar Aalto (in the fifties) and Richard Meier (in the eighties) – have gained commissions for cultural centres and museums by way of open competitions, still held in large numbers. The precedent set by their buildings certainly much influenced German architects and also helped focus discussions at the international level. Probably in no other country are there so many buildings created by architects from elsewhere in Europe and North America. It also seems as if the practice of entrusting ambitious foreign architects with the creation of prestigious buildings in Germany will continue, despite a gradual slowing down in the previous boom. What are the reasons for that ?

Closer consideration of architectural developments in West Germany shows that the reconstruction phase came to an end with the implementation of ambitious cultural edifices. Once post-war society's basic needs had been satisfied with the construction of housing and community facilities (schools, kindergartens, hospitals, civic centres, etc), attention could be devoted to luxury projects such as museums, theatres, and concert halls. After an initial wave of such projects in the late sixties and early seventies, with little foreign involvement, intensive new links were established with international architects as part of the post-modernism debate. That was also facilitated by reductions in travelling-times. Commuting between Helsinki and Wolfsburg still entailed a long day's journey for Alvar Aalto, which he did not take on gladly, whereas nowadays great distances between office and building-site have long been an everyday experience for architects.

So it should come as no surprise that London-based Zaha Hadid, Alvaro Siza from Portugal, and Frank Gehry with an office in California have devised spectacular buildings for the little town of Weil am Rhein. Or that such architects as Giorgio Grassi, Renzo Piano, Daniel Libeskind, and Jean Nouvel are at work in Berlin. In Frankfurt am Main there are buildings by four celebrated Austrian architects (Hans Hollein, Wilhelm Holzbauer, Gustav Peichl, and Friedensreich Hundertwasser). Jacques Herzog and Pierre de Meuron from Switzerland

created a small but much-remarked art gallery in Munich and since then have
won important competitions. English-born Norman Foster is even – to his great
astonishment – rebuilding the Reichstag in Berlin. He himself drew attention
to the fact that the converse situation would be inconceivable in England. –
Just imagine, a German architect replanning facilities at the Palace of Westmin-
ster.

The fact is that Germany has long become an international forum for architecture, and by now hardly any of the world's celebrated architects have not implemented some of their ideas here.

The big building exhibitions, which from the start reckoned with the participation of foreign architects, certainly played an important part there. From the period between the world wars mention must be made of the 1927 Werkbund exhibition in Stuttgart's Weissenhof district, which still attracts architectural
pilgrims from all over the world, eager to look at the homes designed by Le
Corbusier, Victor Bourgeois, Mart Stam, and Josef Frank. In 1957 the Berlin
"Interbau" was on a far larger scale, leading to rebuilding of the war-ravaged
Hansaviertel with the participation of such architects as Alvar Aalto, Jacob Berend Bakema, Luciano Baldessari, and Arne Jacobsen. The model established by
these building exhibitions certainly increased German clients' readiness to
commission architects from outside the country, so it is not surprising that in
this book too over a third of the projects documented entailed foreign involvement.

Despite that however, the opportunities for well-known German architects to
create buildings abroad are somewhat restricted. Among the exceptions are
Oswald Mathias Ungers with the German ambassador's private residence in
Washington, and Josef Paul Kleihues' success in the competition for the Chica-
go museum of contemporary art. Otto Steidle is building in Vienna and Hans
Kollhoff produced a residential block for Rotterdam. Also worthy of mention is
Thomas Herzog's Linz Design-Centre as an important contribution towards innovative ecological architecture, a sphere which will be of increasing importance in decades to come. It should be remembered too that Frei Otto, one of
our age's most imaginative designers, found an outlet for his lightweight constructions in Saudi-Arabia.

The number of examples is quickly exhausted, and none of the younger German
practitioners have as yet received commissions from foreign clients. German architects ultimately suffer from resistance to German influences, which is in turn
the outcome of painful experience or the result of general caution with regard
to threateningly great economic power. Their complaint about not being able to
show what they are capable of abroad will persist so long as acceptance of
non-identified entries to competitions, open to all Europeans, is much greater
in Germany than in other member-states of the European Union. If other countries could increasingly hold architectural competitions open to international
participation, fairer comparison of skills would be possible over the longer
term.

It is to be hoped that the buildings architects produce in Germany during the years to come will continue to contribute towards architectural culture – and not just in aesthetic terms. Recognition and definition of future tasks, resulting from ever greater shortages of resources, will be at least equally important. If solutions are found, the architecture that in this book presents itself in terms of aesthetic ambitions will once again link up with the heroic period of the twenties when architects were aware of both artistic *and* social responsibilities.

Wilfried Wang

Architecture in the Federal Republic of Germany A Historical Outline

● After many years when architecture played only a modest part in public awareness in the Federal Republic of Germany with little coverage in the arts pages of its big daily newspapers, building has once again become an important theme in cultural policy. Today people devote as much enthusiasm to discussing new edifices created by ambitious architects and cherished historic buildings threatened with demolition or in need of extensive restoration as they do to literature, music, and theatre. Architecture has emerged from out of the shadow of mere utilitarianism. Its artistic importance is recognized alongside functionality. This architectural guide presenting 50 buildings aims at documenting how that has increasingly become the case over the past twenty six years. However, a number of very remarkable buildings were also created during the Federal Republic's first years, so this survey of exemplary building in Germany must start with the fifties.

Hans Scharoun:
Philharmonie, Berlin
(1956–63)

Important Architects of the Fifties and Sixties

In a retrospective look at the beginnings of Federal German architecture, much that critical contemporaries denounced as being kitschy and petit-bourgeois is transformed. There is something dance-like and playful, colourful and joyous, about the delicately-dimensioned buildings of the fifties with their rounded corners, curved staircases, and floating roofs. Of course a number of architects, headed by Egon Eiermann and Hans Scharoun, resisted such trends. Eiermann, who was born at Berlin in 1904 and studied with Hans Poelzig, was a central figure during the first quarter century of Federal German architecture. He specialized in industrial and commercial administrative buildings, but also demonstrated high architectural standards in other forms – such as Berlin's Gedächtniskirche (1959-63) whose war-damaged bell-tower he left as a ruin, confronting it with a new hexagonal tower and an octagonal church. This construction was immediately comprehended as a "memorial to bombing-raids" and a critical "symbol of reconstruction". Equally symbolic was the filigrane "German Pavilion", devised together with Sep Ruf, at the 1958 world fair in Brussels. This was optimistically forward-looking as a clear-cut demonstration to other countries that West German architecture was again seeking to link up with the tradition of *New Building*. The worldwide response to that Pavilion secured Eiermann a number of state commissions – such as the new German embassy in Washington (1959-64) and the parliamentary tower in Bonn (1966-69). The latter demonstrates a tendency within his late work towards transparent outer layers of steel-piping, airy balconies, and protection against the sun, set against the voluminous body of the building. Something light and joyous was thus added to the impression of great clarity and strict organization which had always been present in his constructions. This interplay between delicate secondary structure and strict cubes received fullest expression in one of the period's most eloquent edifices, German Olivetti's administrative and training centre in Frankfurt am Main (1969-72).

Egon Eiermann:
Olivetti Building,
Frankfurt am Main
(1969–72)

Eiermann died in July 1970, followed two years later by his most important antipode, Hans Scharoun, born at Bremen in 1893. In his work Scharoun represented the idea of "organic building", involving harmonious relationships between individual aspects of a building and the overall structure. The idea was that form should arise "naturally" out of the task at issue rather than being predetermined by geometrical structures. Eiermann's buildings stand for modernism's optimism that technical progress promises great advances, whereas the representatives of organic architecture were convinced that unsurpassable models of survival were to be found in the organizational structures of nature. Architectural form should thus be the outcome of a process, growing bit by bit, through following a building's inner structure rather than an imposed external form.

Some time passed before the "master of organic form", who worked and taught in Berlin, was able to put his ideas into practice. Many of his prize-winning competition entries in the fifties were not built. Only during the final decade of his life did he manage to implement an admirable late work. Berlin's Philharmonie, viewed as his most important project, was completed in 1963. Out of the idea of music, which also has to be the spatial focus of the concert-experience, Scharoun developed a clearly-structured arena with vineyard-like terraces of spectators around the stage. The success achieved by this building meant that he could now dream up the most unusual of constructions that were nevertheless fulfilled. During the last part of his life there thus came into being a number of important buildings without which the German architectural landscape would be considerably poorer: the Wolfsburg theatre (1965-73), the Shipping Museum at Bremerhaven (1970-75), and the Prussian state library in Berlin (1967-78) which was completed after Scharoun's death under the supervision of his partner Edgar Wisniewski.

The only architects who could escape off-the-peg work were those who remained faithful, despite all opposition, to the high demands they made of their vocation. Their number included Max Taut and Wassili Luckhardt, who were part of the modern architectural avantgarde as early as the twenties, plus the previously-mentioned Sep Ruf and Paul Schneider-Esleben who created the Federal Republic's first multi-storey car-park in 1950 at Düsseldorf. Mention must also be made of Rolf Gutbrot whose beautiful Liederhalle in Stuttgart (1955-56) was acoustically one of the period's best concert-halls. Among the churches built work by Rudolf Schwarz, Dominikus Böhm, Emil Steffann, and Otto Bartning stood out. The parish church of St. Anna at Düren, which is also a place of pilgrimage, was reconstructed (1951-56) from the stones of the mediaeval building destroyed during the war, and this creation by Rudolf and Maria Schwarz provides impressive testimony to the age. Among museums there was Hans Döllgast's architectural rescue-operation on the Alte Pinakothek in Munich (1952-57), taking up the previous structuring of the facade. Inside the long flights of stairs convey the impression that pathos and mourning have been synthesized here in simple and moving fashion.

A New Generation Enters the Field

With the increasing affluence of Federal German society the tasks facing architecture changed as early as the late sixties. In addition a new generation of architects, born after 1920, gradually started to dominate the profession. They created large-scale sports and leisure facilities, civic and congress centres, airports, and satellite towns ready for occupancy whose realization extended far into the seventies. One is almost left with the feeling that the architecture produced to meet the age's characteristic demands comes from another planet. With the big comprehensive schools covering a large catchment area, the shopping centres, the cultural complexes, and the vast university and hospital areas, which today make us shudder, an epoch founded on unlimited belief in progress established a somewhat dubious monument to itself.

Nevertheless even in the seventies there appeared a number of buildings announcing a new architecture. These mostly came from architects who set about developing an unmistakably individual style and implementing it against the predominant trends. Among the pioneers in this architectural development, intended to provide a way out of the dead-end of "building industry functionalism", was Günter Behnisch (b. 1922) whose work followed on, undogmatically and inventively, from the best achievements of modern architecture. The partnership he established at Stuttgart in 1966 was soon entrusted with a project that was to become its best-known work: the sports facilities in Munich's Olympic Park (1968-72) whose sensational tent-like roof construction was discussed across the country. The development of sports halls then became one of the firm's specialities. Spread across the south of Germany are gym and training halls designed by Behnisch, and all of these successfully assert their structural individuality against the laws underlying standardized production. Whether the translucent gym hall at Rothenburg ob der Tauber (1970), standing against the mediaeval town like a delicate veil, or the filigrane sports centre hall at Sulzbach (1984), his work always manifests a wish to breathe individual life into every building despite its rational structure.

While other architects who carried modernism onwards believed at some stage that they had to break with their past and all of a sudden offered pleasant post-modern adornment, Behnisch's buildings remained impressively consistent. He was justly entrusted with planning the plenary and presidential tracts in the new Bonn federal parliament once the politicians had decided to make a provisional seat of government into the federal capital. For almost two decades Behnisch's office struggled with administrators and politicians over transposing a modern democracy's precept of openness into adequate architecture. Finally the architects' sense of quality prevailed, but while the new federal parliament was being constructed between 1987 and 1992 the course of history intervened. After German reunification the Bonn parliament in 1991 decided in favour of Berlin as the new capital.

Two years older than Behnisch is Gottfried Böhm, who in 1952 joined the office of his father, church architect Dominikus Böhm. After the latter's death the

Rudolf Schwarz:
Church of St. Anna, Düren (1951–56)

.Gottfried Böhm:
Pilgrimage Church at Neviges
(1963–68)

son followed in his father's footsteps and initially designed churches character-ized by a formal language reminiscent of Expressionism. This style attained an early high-point in the pilgrimage church at Neviges (1963-68), a small town in the Ruhr which Böhm enriched with triumphantly soaring "alpine architecture" in concrete. This expressive House of God, mighty and rugged like a mountain, seems to exemplify protective monumentality. As early as the sixties, Gottfried Böhm established a highly individual style, very unlike what was being built at that time, so he was viewed as an outsider. His breakthrough only took place during the seventies when European architecture, which had never really seemed unified even though categorized as functionalist, split into the camps of modernism and post-modernism. Since then Böhm and a number of other ar-chitects who upheld artistic independence have no longer been viewed as indi-vidualists but rather as trailblazers of "post-modern" architecture propagated in the Federal Republic by Heinrich Klotz, the first director of the German Archi-tecture Museum. That paid off and the former church architect was entrusted with a number of much-remarked large-scale projects for the IBA (International Building Exhibition 1984/87) in Berlin, public authorities, and well-endowed companies.

Oswald Mathias Ungers, the man who designed the German Architecture Museum at Frankfurt am Main (1979-84), is six years younger than Gottfried Böhm. After gaining his diploma with Egon Eiermann, Ungers established his own office in 1950 and produced residential buildings. They included his own house in the Lindenthal district of Cologne (1958-59) where the somewhat restless structure is calmed by way of a clinker brick wall. Unlike most of his colleagues, Ungers was increasingly troubled by the great discrepancy between architectural ambitions and the reality of construction. So in the mid-sixties he withdrew for over a decade from the hurly-burly of building and concentrated on the development of his own theory of architecture and on teaching. During this time a number of important competition projects came into being, includ-ing his plans for the German embassy in the Vatican (1965) and for the Wallraf-Richartz museum at Cologne (1975). There thus matured an individual style which resisted functionalism's levelling down of architectural inventiveness. Since the eighties Ungers' idea of architecture has received expression in large-scale projects, as exemplified by the striking high-rise complex on Frankfurt's trade fair site (1983-84).

Foreign architects, known far beyond their own countries, have increasingly made a contribution towards building in the Federal Republic that was to satis-fy high demands and endow architecture with new self-assurance. The fact that in the eighties a museum-building boom got under way, allowing architects great artistic freedom, also accorded with local authorities' wish to give "big names" a chance of implementing their idiosyncratic ideas in German cities. It was Hans Hollein, born at Vienna in 1934 and one of the most consistent of commuters between art, design, and architecture, who was accorded the pleas-ure of launching the new museum architecture. Hollein first made a name for himself as an unconventional interior designer. He entered big-time building with the commission to plan Mönchengladbach's Abteiberg museum.

Hollein's architecture demonstrates autonomy without the least claim to monumentality alongside the impressive exhibits in this collection. Architecture critic Wolfgang Pehnt has spoken of this Abteiberg museum being a "masterpiece of collage", which reacted to the surrounding conglomeration of buildings from different centuries with an ensemble of diverse structures and materials rather than a unified edifice. Only the vertical administrative building – with an unusually structured facade – dominates the museum site. The exhibition rooms are built into the hillside and reached by way of a little temple, standing on its own, that takes the visitor down into the main area. Inside one feels well looked after and gladly follows the diagonals indicating, rather than directing, a way through the exhibits.

If mention should be made of another museum that like Mönchengladbach sparked off a mini-revolution and enormously provoked public discussion of architecture, then it must certainly be Stuttgart's Staatsgalerie (1977-83), designed by James Stirling, born at Glasgow in 1926. This marked the appearance on the Federal German scene of a globally celebrated architect who had long endeavoured to work in this country. The Stuttgart museum was the first of his projects to be built in Germany. However, anyone who previously only knew Stirling from the somewhat aloof university buildings at Leicester and Cambridge was considerably shocked by architecture teeming with historical citations. Of course German architectural critics mocked the project's strident postmodernism and misunderstood Stirling's good-natured humour as pure cynicism. Yet Stirling had only wittily and imaginatively further developed Hollein's ideas about architectural landscaping.

Beyond the Big Cities

Most of the buildings presented here are in big cities, but that does not mean the German provinces completely lack ambitious architecture. Two examples from the south of the country prove the contrary: Eichstätt an der Altmühl and Weil am Rhein. During the past decade the little Bavarian episcopal and university town of Eichstätt, once only known to insiders, has become a real place of pilgrimage for architects. Nowhere else in Germany is there a town that offers such exemplary demonstration of appropriate dealings with historic buildings. The architecturally fruitful dialogue between past and present is dominated by Karljosef Schattner (b. 1924), who as university and diocese architect has shaped Eichstätt for over thirty years.

There is thus much to be discovered here. That starts with the education faculty at the Catholic university (1960-67) whose strictly-structured facades reveal a skeletal style of building with undressed stone walls, and continues with the theological library (1978-80) incorporated in the baroque "Ulmer Hof"

Hans Döllgast:
Alte Pinakothek, Munich
(1952–57)

O. M. Ungers
German Architecture Museum
Frankfurt am Main (1979–84)

viewed through green protective glass as in an aquarium. Mention must also be made of the diocesan museum (1977-82), also involving rebuilding, where the old roof truss is underpinned by a new steel construction, and of the institute of psychology (1985-88) whose modern northerly facade is installed in front of the house walls of two 16th century buildings.

The list of buildings is long but they are linked by Schattner's dealings with history. Neither conserving nor restoring, his architectural methods admirably exemplify an attempt at carefully preserving the old while adding new utilizations, but at the same time presenting new buildings as uncompromisingly as possible. Schattner's aesthetic theory culminates in the idea of contrasting different materials and forms of construction. The link between old and new is sought in shared entrances and staircases, but never enforced through unifying structure. Steel and glass are used time and again as genuinely modern materials, which are easily identified as new components and allow the historical nature of old buildings to stand out all the more clearly. It is through love of detailing that Schattner's new buildings establish links with the craftsmanship of the past but without seeking to ingratiate themselves come what may. At any rate the outcome is reconciliation of modernism with that traditional architecture it once sought to displace completely.

In Weil am Rhein, close to the Swiss border in the south of Baden-Württemberg, we are confronted with a completely different phenomenon. Here the client is not some tradition-conscious bishop but a modern businessman. Neither is there a single architect who covers a town with his buildings. Instead there are several creators, viewed as being part of the international avantgarde, whose striking ideas make an unusual contribution to a big company's image. It may not be anything new for firms to turn to ambitious architects and to step out of line compared with all those enterprises satisfied with mass-produced worthy industrial architecture. What is unusual is that Vitra did not want to restrict itself to a single, easily recognizable architectural style, but instead commissioned a series of highly idiosyncratic architects to devise production halls, administrative centres, and other buildings on a company site that by now looks like a small architectural exhibition rather than a commercial zone.

The opportunity for this exceptional development was offered by an extensive fire which in 1981 destroyed over half the production capacity. A start was made in the same year with erection of the new factory halls designed by English-born Nicholas Grimshaw, who shortly afterwards attracted international attention with his contribution to the Aztec West industrial park near Bristol (1983). In 1989 a new factory hall and the Vitra design museum were created in the ideas-workshop of Frank O. Gehry from California. His bizarrely sculpted museum building is one of the few projects which entered architectural history shortly after completion. Two more new buildings were inaugurated on the site in 1993: the "deconstructionist" station for the firm's fire brigade, devised by Zaha M. Hadid who teaches at London's famous Architectural Association, and a conference pavilion with which Tadao Ando from Japan wanted to establish a symbol of tranquillity creating a thrilling contrast with Gehry's agitated formal language. Another production hall, produced by Alvaro Siza, the best-known Portuguese architect in Germany, began operations in 1994.

A Look at the Nineties

While Behnisch, Böhm, Ungers, Josef Paul Kleihues, and such younger architects as Fritz Auer and Karlheinz Weber, Meinhard von Gerkan, and Volkwin Marg continued to produce "late works", buildings by people born in the forties increasingly dominated public interest. Among the outstanding practitioners was Thomas Herzog who during the sixties gained experience in the office of Peter von Seidlein and then set up on his own in 1971. Five years later he designed the much-extolled "Haus Burghardt" near Regensburg, a wedge-shaped structure of wood and glass rising out of the ground whose architectural form is both the product of idiosyncratic ideas about structure and a function of a logical energy-saving concept, minimizing the house's heating needs by way of passive utilization of solar energy, controlled ventilation processes, and careful insulation. Herzog's starting-point involved making our age's ecological demands into essential parameters within his design, but always in such a way that the most recent energy technologies are surprisingly transformed into architecture.

Axel Schultes and Otto Steidle, both born in 1943, represent two other unmistakable positions within today's architecture. At a time when people have become ever more sceptical about prefabricated building, the latter has stood up for the possibilities still very much available to creative deployment of standardized components, inviting the user to make personal adaptations. He proved that at the start of the seventies when he attracted attention with highly unconventional housing in Munich and Nuremberg. These are more like larger than life-size industrial shelving made of concrete supports, "filled in" with big window-areas and prefabricated wall-elements, than normal housing. In his larger-scale projects Steidle also offers users a chance of taking active possession of this architecture. It may be wrong to maintain that the Gruner & Jahr publishing building in Hamburg, jointly devised with Uwe Kiessler and completed in 1991, is provisional architecture, but the architects developed a lively structure composed of small-scale elements which adapt flexibly to changing functional demands and the needs of the people working there.

Axel Schultes – in successful partnership with Dietrich Bangert, Bernd Jansen, and Stefan Scholz between 1974 and 1991 – first implemented a number of interesting projects for Berlin and also the "Schirn" cultural centre in Frankfurt am Main (1980-86) before establishing his own office in 1992. That was made possible by work on the Bonn Art Museum (1985-92), one of the most remarkable buildings of the past ten years. Hardly any other museum looks so striking and yet at the same time outstandingly serves the works of art exhibit-

Karljosef Schattner:
Institute of Psychology, Eichstätt
(1985–88)

Thomas Herzog:
Haus Burghardt, Regensburg
(1976)

ed there. Both the outer and inner rooms, created by Schultes for art and its public, are bright and light, but they also possess a degree of congenial monumentality. The Bonn building teaches its visitors astonishment not fear; it does not oppress them. One feels that the architect has a talent for devising rooms in which an impression of tranquillity calms the excited big-city soul. Maybe it was that quality which led Helmut Kohl to decide in favour of Axel Schultes when faced with two equal winners in the 1995 competition for a new federal chancellor's office in Berlin.

Berlin as New Federal Capital

If one wants to speculate about architecture's immediate future, the answer is that it has already begun in Berlin. That got under way in summer 1991 when the German federal parliament decided that Berlin should be the new capital of a reunited Germany and the seat of the federal government. Moving a country's capital is a very unusual business, further intensified in this case by the fact that for over forty years this city was divided into two hostile territories and social systems. Such a competitive situation meant that there were striking differences between the two parts of the city, especially with regard to urban planning and architecture.

As early as 1957 the difference between the systems was made into an urban development programme with the opening in West Berlin of the International Building Exhibition (Interbau for short). The idea was that the power and productivity of Federal German democracy should be vividly demonstrated in the form of progressive housing – as compared with the false pomp of East Berlin's Stalinallee and deficiencies of administration in the communist GDR. Chosen for that task was the old, densely-built Hansaviertel, which had been almost completely destroyed during the war. Any well-known modern architect was represented in the Hansaviertel with a building. Almost thirty years later, after development of a new conception of city-planning, exemplified in the idea of "urban repairs", the West Berlin Senate once again decided to hold an International Building Exhibition (IBA). Its director, Josef Paul Kleihues, declared that reconstruction of a city destroyed first by bombs and then by planners' ignorance entailed a new model of urban planning. This involved establishing modern housing on the old city ground-plan, retaining the block-structure while gutting inner areas and embellishing them with green oases for the public.

West Berlin thus sought – with help from internationally celebrated architects – to make itself more attractive, while in the East old buildings became increasingly run-down and the terrible monotony of prefabricated settlements spread ever further. The reunited city was thus faced with the great problem of step-by-step restoration of economic, social, and architectural balance in its two completely disparate parts. That and the task of moving governmental functions to Berlin will occupy the city beyond the start of the new millenium. A new architectural trend can already be seen. For forty years architects such as Egon Eiermann and Günter Behnisch endowed the Federal Republic with un-bombastic buildings whose constructive elegance and transparency captivate, but in recent years a public dispute has flared up over the new Berlin architecture that no longer shuns monumental gestures. That development is symbolized by the decision to house the new federal parliament in its predecessor, the old Reichstag building. The fact that an English architect, Norman Foster, was chosen to equip this awe-inspiring building for its new task may be seen as a reassuring message to other countries.

Norman Foster:
Plan for reconstruction
of the Berlin Reichstag
(1995-)

Further Reading:

Durth, Werner and Gutschow, Niels (1987): *Nicht wegwerfen ! Architektur und Städtebau der fünfziger Jahre,* German National Committee for Conservation, Bonn

Feldmeyer, Gerhard G. (1993): *Die Neue Deutsche Architektur,* with an introduction by Manfred Sack, Stuttgart

Hackelsberger, Christoph (1985): *Die aufgeschobene Moderne. Ein Versuch zur Einordnung der Architektur der fünfziger Jahre,* Munich/Berlin

Jaeger, Falk (Ed.) (1985): *Bauen in Deutschland. Ein Führer durch die Architektur des 20. Jahrhunderts in der Bundesrepublik und in West-Berlin,* Stuttgart

Klotz, Heinrich (1987): *Moderne und Postmoderne. Architektur der Gegenwart 1960-1980,* Brunswick/Wiesbaden

Lampugnani, Vittorio M. (Ed.) (1983): *Hatje-Lexikon der Architektur des 20. Jahrhunderts,* Stuttgart

Pehnt, Wolfgang (1983): *Der Anfang der Bescheidenheit. Kritische Aufsätze zur Architektur des 20. Jahrhunderts,* Munich

Thomsen, Christian W. (1991): *Experimentelle Architekten der Gegenwart,* Cologne

The Other Architecture: Building in the GDR

Gerd Zimmermann

● This book describes 50 buildings constructed in Germany during the past 26 years. Nothing could be found in the former GDR that was as aesthetically worthwhile as the work of such architects as Behnisch, Herzog, or Schattner. The buildings erected were for the most part counter-images rather than models.

Of course, compared with the plenary chamber in the federal parliament at Bonn, the Palace of the Republic in East Berlin is a banal prefabricated work whose late-modern style was as widespread in the seventies as sand on a beach. East German economics of scarcity, cultural indoctrination, and extensive undermining of building traditions left their mark on both "state architecture" and collectivist mass settlements. The fundamental psycho-political damage done entailed far-reaching suppression of subjectivity and to a certain extent the elimination of architects, leading to rampantly faceless and inexpressive buildings.

Nevertheless, one must be careful not to make the aesthetic judgement surreptitiously passed on GDR architecture an instrument of one-sided repression and exclusion. After all, what is to prevent the Palace of the Republic, which is not conspicuously worse than other congress centres, from being incorporated in a new and vital context ?

GDR architecture is not non-architecture. Our initial thesis is that this is a *different* German architecture. And that architecture is not identical with its stereotypes. It involved specific preconditions and a face of its own. Despite all the centralized state's suppression and oppression, there did exist creative niches – in students' "paper architecture", the construction of churches, and work involving historical monuments. To a certain extent it can be said that the GDR formed its own concept of architecture. As the architecture of a different society it thus challenges a comparison which would throw light on different patterns of value in West and East as expressed in building.

In addition architecture in the GDR can in no way be viewed in isolation as a singular phenomenon. It can only be explained as the outcome of a specific geo-political constellation: on the one hand bound up in the structure of the socialist block and also localized on the borderline of East-West confrontation; and, on the other, rooted in a shared German history and oriented towards developments in the Federal Republic and Western Europe. GDR architecture thus participated, despite all its particular characteristics, in contemporary architectural trends to a high degree. At second glance, a remarkable convergence between architectural development in the two Germanies also becomes apparent. So let us endeavour to make at least a broad attempt at interpreting GDR architecture in that context.

City destroyed by war (1945)

Soviet Palace, Moscow
(project 1933)

The Fifties: Between Traditionalism and Modernism

For the Federal Republic the years between 1947 and 1965 were the time of reconstruction and the economic miracle. Those were key years for its state of political and cultural health. The foundations for unprecedented economic growth and comprehensive modernization were established with the Marshall Plan, currency reform, and finally setting up of the Federal Republic. That is one aspect, accompanied by a big building boom and incentives for architecture and design whose model – it seems worth emphasizing – was clearly the USA.

The other aspect points to a remarkable weakness in the period's intellectual culture. Comparing the post-war period in the Federal Republic with the twenties, Jost Hermand even comes to the conclusion that cultural insubstantiality prevailed, deeply rooted in lack of a genuine social impulse towards renewal.[1]

It is worth mentioning that the motivation for adapting the formal language of modernism – for which the Thyssen high-rise building (architects: Hentrich and Petschnigg, 1955) is an early and celebrated example in the Federal Republic – involved economic functionalism rather than the objectives of social reform. For the early moderns of the twenties, however, social utopias were of fundamental importance.

On the other hand the spirit of the age certainly played a part there since in the awareness of contemporaries, East as well as West Germans, the free, joyous, colourful forms of fities designs symbolized an escape from the sombre wartime period with nights of bombing and taking refuge in cellars. Against that background the age's Italy cult – the attraction of the sunny South and "la dolce vita", which also left traces in architecture – becomes comprehensible. Hermann Glaser speaks in that connection of the "economic miracle style".[2]

The 1957 International Building Exhibition (Interbau) in West Berlin, the "shop-window of the free world", was intended to provide "a clear-cut declaration by Western architecture" in favour of modern forms, serving as the Western answer to the already constructed Stalinallee in East Berlin. Interbau, like much other post-war planning, followed the model of a structured and diversified city whose origins lay in Third Reich planning for the post-war period.[3]

Early architectural developments in the Soviet Zone of Occupation first involved – as throughout Germany – a time of desire for reconstruction and "dreams in the ruins", uniting collapse and a visionary yearning for renewal. Plans were thus dominated by rejection of the old 19th century city, dismissed as being chaotic and unhygienic. The destruction of cities was basically also viewed as a chance for new and modern developments. In what was known as the "collective plan" for Berlin, for example, this kind of criticism of the big city, urging de-urbanization and following on from twenties' ideas about garden cities and settlements, led to a proposal for complete replanning of Berlin. The situation up to 1949 can be described as comparatively pluralistic. There was no binding programme but rather divergent views about planning and architecture, extending from the modernists to the traditionalists.[4]

East German architectural development experienced a radical, ideologically-motivated turning-point in 1950, a year after establishment of the Federal Republic and the GDR – and thus of two German states – and escalation of the Cold War. In 1950 a delegation headed by Reconstruction Minister Bolz travelled to Moscow and returned with a programme that was made into the guideline for GDR architecture through the "Reconstruction Law" and the "16 Principles of Urban Development". Neo-classical monumentality, to some extent an imitation of Stalinist architecture, was meant to symbolize the new authority and to support the staging of mass parades on main thoroughfares and big squares.[5] This "architecture of national traditions" became a formative and binding concept in the GDR until the mid-fifties, and the best-known outcome of this campaign was Berlin's neo-classical Stalinallee. The programmatic slogan for the opening of this architecture was "National in Form – Socialist in Content".

Stalinallee,
East Berlin's
main thoroughfare
(1952–58)

What were the motives for this development, which was accompanied by defamation of modernism and the Bauhaus, making them taboo?

Firstly, the Stalinallee was seen as a demonstration of reconstruction in the East German capital. Following on from the Soviet idea of the "residential palace", subsidized public housing was also to be refined – to some degree as a socialization of the feudal.

Secondly, the bombast of neo-classicism, already widely conventionalized as a sign of power, served the representation of authority in two ways: as self-stylization and a setting-off of the GDR against the modernist and cosmopolitan West, and as an architectural token of submissiveness to the Soviet occupiers – architecture in the service of the class struggle and power politics.

Thirdly, this architecture, like traditionalism in building in the Western zones, fed off subliminal continuation of the basic pattern of architecture during the Third Reich – both regional protection of local styles and neo-classical state architecture à la Speer.

Fourthly, the Stalinallee was intended to establish a signal for a *national architecture,* a new *German* architecture, which opposed the cosmopolitanism of the international style in architecture. As late as 1954, Hermann Henselmann, the outstanding figure in GDR architecture, stated, directing his message towards West German colleagues: "The precondition for the struggle for unity of our fatherland is that we persist with depiction of our national character in contemporary buildings, making that a priority, and decisively resist all efforts to downgrade our cities into soulless, cosmopolitan constructions".[6]

The idea of a completely new "socialist" city was first implemented with Stalinstadt (later Eisenhüttenstadt). The new city came into being as a totally planned structure in conjunction with the new iron foundry. The main thoroughfare ran directly to the works, bringing the skyline of blast furnaces

"Residential Palace", Stalinallee,
East Berlin (1952-58)

and smoking chimneys into the cityscape – with the city structure as a meta-phor for the pathos of industrial work and a celebration of workers.

Stalinallee in East Berlin and Interbau in West Berlin were so-to-speak imple-mentations of architectural manifestos to the right and left of the Iron Curtain. The 20th century dispute between traditionalists and modernists, which domi-nated the twenties and latently permeated the Third Reich, returned in the fif-ties as a symbol of East-West confrontation and incorporation of the two Ger-man states in the victor-powers' spheres of influence. There thus came into being Stalinist-influenced architecture in the East and U.S.-inspired modernism in the West.

The Sixties: Techno-Vision and Social Utopia

The neo-historicism and monumentalism in GDR architecture, particularly between 1950 and 1955, entailed considerable ambivalence. On the one hand, this architecture was supposed to be endowed with expressive and symbolic power, very much akin to *architecture parlante,* while, on the other, that ambi-tion was smothered by the primitive and kitschy nature of Stalinist architectu-ral motifs.

In addition, architecture was undermined by great divergences between stat-us and function. Right from the beginnings of the GDR that was apparent as a characteristic social symptom with a fatal dualism between, on the one hand, status architecture for state and party (with central axis, big square, and promi-nent buildings) and, on the other, collectivistic mass housing in socialist resi-dential complexes. Here "state architecture" with a somewhat kitschy upstart aesthetic and prestige, and there "everyday architecture" characterized by highly primitive functionality.

Criticism of monstrous prestige architecture got under way in the Soviet Un-ion within a year of Stalin's death, and in 1955 the GDR also made a start on officially abjuring such buildings. The criticism leading to this turning-point mainly attacked "over-valuation of architecture's conceptual basis" and lack of interest in possible economies because of adherence to craft methods.

Radical industrialization of building in the GDR then got under way on the basis of standardization, mass production, and prefabricated construction. De-velopment from 1957 of the "socialist city of Hoyerswerda" served as a proto-type (ignoring twenties' precursors) and demonstrated the consequences: re-duction of architecture to the production principles of panels, slabs, and cranes. Previously the classical model had been ideologized and made into a dogma; now industrial technology became a fetish.

To be sure, in its technocratic emphases from the start of the sixties the GDR largely followed the model of Western economic functionalism and euphoria over technological progress. That also received expression in mass housing in satellite towns (for instance Halle-Neustadt from 1964 and extensions of Ros-tock), reconstruction of town centres following a concept that gave primacy to the car, and the forms of interchangeable prefabricated architecture. The parallels with international – and particularly Federal German – architectural developments (residential fortresses in concrete and city office silos) are unmistakable here. Attempts were frequently made to compensate for the inexpressiveness of the architecture by the application of art as for example with the "House of the Teacher" in Berlin.

Sixties satellite town: Rostock

A concept that had much shaped the fifties persisted in the following decade. The "anarchy" of the capitalist city was countered by a striving for *harmonization of ensemble* and *the significance of* "City Crowns". The fictitious social intent of such ensembles was explained in terms of the architectural status of the "socialist human community". It was thus expected that architecture should be a medium for social utopia, while the urban ensemble in practice served the self-presentation of party, state, and economic officialdom. Once again it was Hermann Henselmann, one of the architects of the Stalinallee who planned and also to some extent implemented "City Crowns" as central tall buildings in Berlin and various GDR regional centres: the Zeiss high-rise edifice in Jena (shaped like a telescope), the Berlin television tower ("Signals Tower"), etc.[7] The symbolism displayed in these buildings is incredibly simple: a telescope for Jena's optical industry, a high-rise building as a sail in the harbour city of Rostock, a hexagon for Magdeburg, the city that manufactures heavy machinery, etc.[8]

Interesting as social utopias, and also in comparison with Western projects, were plans for "large-scale socialist residential units" bringing together ideas from Le Corbusier's *unité d'habitation* and Soviet communal houses from the twenties. The sixties "thaw" made some attempts at reform and modernization generally possible in the GDR, despite the Wall. Architectural innovations – there were a few – were both technological (development of such new building systems as mesh and shell constructions, processes which did not previously exist in the GDR) and social (where at least greater theoretical attention was devoted to sociological and psychological aspects of the built environment, e.g. in connection with "discussion of monotony").

The degree to which theoretical discussion was still blocked can, however, be demonstrated in the continued tabooing of the Bauhaus, which had been passed over in silence since 1950 even though acceptance would have provided arguments for industrial building. From this one can see that the guidelines of 1950 still had a hold on at least top officials.

At the start of the seventies the housing construction programme was launched as the "core of the welfare programme". This was urgently necessary in social terms, but it led to the monotony of prefabricated construction and ultimately to enslavement of architectural thinking as a whole.

Even though systemic shortcomings accompanied the GDR from the start, one can venture to say that stifling of the sixties' reforms made stagnation unstoppable. While reforms in the Federal Republic left traces, in the GDR with its restrictions on freedom of expression and opinion certain discussions did not

Modernization
of the centre of East Berlin
(1961-64)

occur or were completely emasculated. Just consider the theme of entanglement in Nazism. In the West a start was made on facing up to this, whereas the situation in the GDR remained highly contradictory. On the one hand, anti-fascism seemed to be a fundamental state dogma, personally attested to by the fate suffered by the country's leaders, but, on the other, the extent of willing complicity, in both word and deed, was hushed up. The fact that Third Reich architecture was a taboo theme in the GDR says much. There were no extended studies of this topic – just a few discussions which were not publicized. One of the reasons for that silence probably involves shying away from explanation of why the phenomenology of Stalinist and Nazi architecture was so similar. Investigating Nazi architecture would inevitably have led to discussion of totalitarianism in both systems.

In the seventies, which will not be further considered here, the social aspect of house-construction degenerated into the dogma of prefabricated building, also revealing the ambivalence of architecture as a concept imposed from above. In the construction of mass housing ideally everyone gets at least minimal accomodation, but that also entails organization of depersonalization of the individual and deprivation of a voice. Prefabricated panelling, which shows nothing, thus becomes a vehicle for unlimited banalization, and at the same time an instrument for coy privatization behind standardization.

Later expansion of Berlin as a showpiece capital was vigorously pursued at the cost of increasing decay in the provinces, so that the architectural gulf between luxurious prestige at the centre and purified functionality on the periphery – palace and hut – became apparent. In the authority responsible for special building, later called the "Berlin general building directorate", the political class's addiction to status became institutionalized.

The Eighties: Adornment of Crisis

In the Federal Republic, it may be assumed, specific demands by the 68 generation were converted into more lasting social solutions – for instance, the occupation and renovation of empty houses which then became an element in cautious urban renewal. Rebellion against large-scale demolition brought about a new acceptance of organically developed architecture together with demands for participation and individual involvement. Careful urban renovation, as finally adopted as a programme by the IBA in Berlin, also signified taking into account criticism of modernistic city development.

Commitment to old towns and preservation of historically valuable buildings also increased in the GDR. However, the bureaucracy and prefabricated units (as the former's technological substratum) turned out to be incapable of change.

The ecological debate with its fundamental consequences for architecture provides another example. This was largely absent in the GDR and when such topics were discussed was even made a criminal offence.

Totalitarian structures therefore led to suspension of public debate about alternatives, and this impoverishment is readily apparent. Thus viewed, the eighties are the decade of mere adornment of an unstoppable crisis. In architecture that resulted in a superficial "post-modernism" founded on ideological servitude.

While the GDR production line unceasingly churned out prefabricated units and building blocks, it made the concession of decoration in the face of prevalent monotony. Panels were adorned with nostalgic embellishments or tilted to produce mansard roofs. So instead of the model being fundamentally changed it was only meagrely beautified.

Palace of the Republic, East Berlin (1973–76)

The historicism that returned to architecture after the early fifties exerted the same kind of impact. On the one hand the historic originals degenerated or were removed, while on the other historicising "prefabricated baroque" ornamentation appeared as a reconciliation with breaches in history. That inevitably ended in kitsch, as demonstrated in Berlin's Friedrichstadtpalast.

Such attempts at "prettification" could not counter decline, which was rooted much deeper in the political and bureaucratic system's incapacity to reform itself. In architecture that ultimately led to extensive undermining of architects, the progressive decay of old towns, and brutalization of new building.

Since 1989, with the end of the GDR and reunification of Germany, the situation facing architecture is absolutely contradictory. On the one side building has been liberated from the stigma of an economics of scarcity and predominance of the prefabricated. Historic old towns are being renovated and highly cultivated new architecture – such as Peter Kulka's parliament building for Saxony – is appearing.

On the other hand, we witness the eager exporting and importing of long-antiquated Western models of settlement, which clash with ecological necessities and result in chaotic breaking-up of landscapes through haphazard commercial and residential construction, and in the destruction of historic buildings. What is required is a modern *architecture of simplicity* according with ecological principles.

Such a programme will scarcely be able to follow directly on from GDR architecture. However, far from any nostalgia, we in East Germany will be able to take up a culture of modesty that grew in niches – and also the idea of well-devised prefabrication. That is of current interest provided it is not cheaply put into practice, following the model of large-scale construction-units, but instead is applied in "intelligent" products within co-ordinated semi-finished industrial fabrication. A look back at the GDR can thus also stimulate new beginnings.

Notes

1. Cf. Durth, Werner and Gutschow, Niels (1987): *Nicht wegwerfen! Architektur und Städtebau der 50er Jahre,* German National Committee for Conservation, Bonn

2. Glaser, Hermann (1986): *Kulturgeschichte der Bundesrepublik Deutschland 1949-1967,* Vol. 2, Munich/Vienna

3. Durth, Werner and Gutschow, Niels, op cit, pp. 24-37, and Lammert, P: *Die gegliederte und aufgelockte Stadt vor und nach 1945. Eine Skizze zur Planungsgeschichte,* in: Die Alte Stadt 14/1987, No. 4, pp. 352-66

4. Cf. Schätzke, Andreas (1991): *Zwischen Bauhaus und Stalinallee. Architekturdiskussion im östlichen Deutschland 1945-55,* Bauwelt Fundamente 95, Brunswick/Wiesbaden

5. Cf. Hain, Simone (1993): *Reise nach Moskau: Erste Betrachtungen zur politischen Struktur des städtebaulichen Leitbildwandels des Jahres 1950 in der DDR,* in: Wiss. Zeitschr. d. Hochschule für Architektur und Bauwesen Weimar 39/1993 No. 1/2

6. Henselmann, Hermann (1978): *Probleme des Städte- und Wohnungsbaus* (Lecture at the second local authorities conference, Dresden 1954), in: ibid., *Gedanken, Ideen, Bauten, Projekte,* Berlin

7. It is nonetheless interesting how early Expressionist visions of a great unified building (of which the Bauhaus dreamed and which were proclaimed in Bruno Taut's *Stadtkrone* – City Crown) were first transmogrified in the Soviet Palace project (from 1931) and then in the GDR sixties experienced a trivial postlude, long overtaken by reality.

8. Cf. Flierl, Bruno (1979): *Zur sozialistischen Architekturentwicklung in der DDR. Theoretische Probleme und Analysen der Praxis,* Bauakademie der DDR, Institut für Städtebau und Architektur, Berlin

Architect: Alvar Aalto, Helsinki
Planning: Harald Deilmann, Düsseldorf
Elissa Aalto, Helsinki (artistic adviser)
Building: Aalto Theatre, Essen
Location: Essen Stadtgarten (Rellinghauser Straße)
Client: Gemeinnützige Theater-Baugesellschaft Essen mbH
Construction: 1983-1987

Alvar Aalto

● The city of Essen had to wait a long time for its exceptional theatre. Even though Alvar Aalto's design far outshone other entries in the 1959 competition, this building only opened in September 1988 after a planning process extending over thirty years. Within five years of the competition the architect submitted his final plans with the characteristic two-level roof construction and the integrated stage-tower. However, lack of public money prevented implementation of the project. After a long period of revisions to the plan, the Finnish architect, one of the most important trailblazers in New Building, died in 1976. Nevertheless, Essen persisted in its wish to go ahead with this project and in 1981 entrusted planning to Harald Deilmann with Elissa Aalto as artistic adviser. His task was to reconcile changed building regulations and functional aspects of the new theatre with the original plan. Aalto once said that his work was inspired by "primal ideas". With the Essen theatre these ideas were derived from the amphitheatres of classical antiquity, and Aalto devised a steeply-raked auditorium arousing the impression of being part of a circular area that incorporates what is happening on stage.

Together with the hall's stylishly asymetrical form and the undulation of the higher-level seating, that gives rise to an almost intimate space, atmospheric even when only half full. High-quality design also plays a part there, evident in the detailing of furnishings, lighting, door-handles, and stairways. In Aalvo's interpretation the aesthetics of the fifties, expressed in this radiant building's pale granite, seem timeless, captivating us with their great charm and expressiveness.

Further reading:
Elissa Aalto, *Essen theatre,* in: ARKKITEHTI – Finnish Architectural Journal, 2/1989, p. 34-41

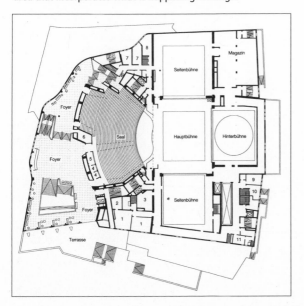

Architect: Tadao Ando, Osaka
Planning: Günter Pfeifer & Roland Mayer, Lörrach
Building: Conference and Meeting Centre
Location: Vitra company area, Weil am Rhein
Client: Vitra GmbH
Construction: 1992-1993

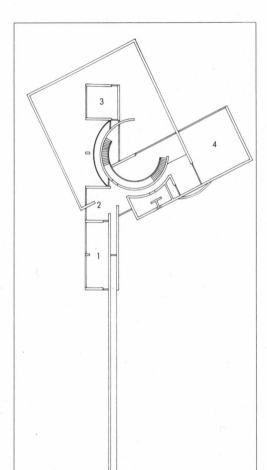

● In Weil am Rhein, a little town close to the frontier with Switzerland, a committed business man has established a monument to the international architectural avantgarde of our time. Tadao Ando was thus enabled to plan his first building outside Japan – close to Frank O. Gehry's spectacular Vitra Design Museum. The Osaka architect was faced with the task of devising a tranquil place for conferences and trainings with a large seminar room, a library, recreational facilities, and smaller rooms. The outcome was a meditative pavilion construction with the aura of a small monastery school, protected by a long wall from the explosive impact of the neighbouring museum.

Tadao Ando (b.1941), a self-taught architect who in 1985 was awarded the Alvar Aalto medal for his work, demonstrates real mastery in his use of concrete. In Germany this material is made responsible for all the constructional sins of recent decades, but the Japanese think highly of it. In Japan concrete is used with such awareness of quality that plastering is unnecessary since the mould creates patterning as a surface structure for facades. The conference building at Weil also lives from the sculptural nature of this material, and the light unified walls act as an ideal reflector of surrounding nature.

Tadao Ando has responded to Gehry's architecture of anarchistic movement with a building of disciplined tranquillity. Its formal austerity and low elevation, achieved through putting one floor underground, allow the building to fit harmoniously – despite its aesthetic idiosyncrasy, asserted in windowless facades – into an old cherry orchard.

Further Reading:
Tadao Ando, *Konferenzpavillon in Weil am Rhein,* in: DAM Architektur Jahrbuch 1994, pp. 58-63

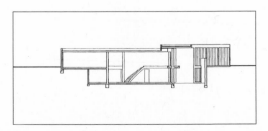

Architects: Auer + Weber, Munich
Building: District Administrative Centre, Starnberg
Location: Münchner Straße, Starnberg
Client: Starnberg District Council
Construction: 1985-1987

Fritz Auer, Carlo Weber

● The Starnberg district administrative centre – whose architects won the 1989 German Architecture prize – is situated close to Lake Starnberg, between the town and a thirties water sports development. The latter's pyramid roofs and the extended flat-roofed boathouses influenced a plan sparked off by the attractive interplay between shoreline, river, and surrounding buildings. The natural landscape, water, and sky are the elements to which the building's materials, forms of construction, and colours relate – as in the transparent outer facade with its shimmering bluish-green components, the metallic roof covering which adapts to the changing colours of the sky, and the skeletal construction utilizing unpainted wood. The clarity of the wooden construction, the links between buildings and landscape, the garden-design, the transition from what is enclosed to openness, and of course the roof formations are all ultimately also influenced by traditional Japanese architecture. The individual areas of the district administrative centre are similarly grouped, demonstrating a graceful geometry, around an open courtyard garden, while the wooden skeleton of the two-storey, highly structured building is based on a strict and constant ground-plan.

As students Fritz Auer and Carlo Weber gained practical experience in Günter Behnisch's then newly-established office where they later worked as partners from 1966 to 1979, playing an important part in such big projects as the Munich Olympic buildings and initial plans for the federal parliament in Bonn. In 1980 they became independent and established their own office, which has since enriched the German architectural landscape with such impressive constructions as the Helen Keller secondary school in Munich (1988-93) and the theatre at Hof (1990-94).

Further Reading:
Landratsamt Starnberg, in: Baumeister 10/1988, pp. 44-53

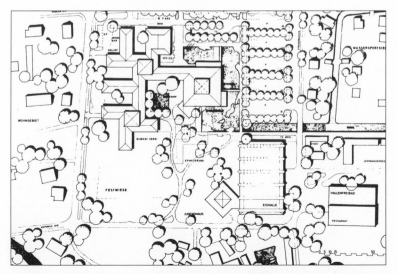

Architects: Behnisch & Partners, Stuttgart
Roofing: Behnisch & Partners, Frei Otto, Leonhardt + Andrä
Building: Buildings and site for the XX. Olympic Games
Client: Olympia-Baugesellschaft GmbH
Construction: 1968-1972

cussion even among non-architects. The concept of an Olympic landscape necessitated development of innovative roofing, providing a harmonious counterpoint to organic natural forms. A tent-form seemed ideal for that, particularly in relationship to the unusual panoramic view of Alpine peaks. In addition the association with a circus tent offered a suitable response to the prescribed motto of "joyous games". The translucent tent-landscape of Munich's Olympic buildings, more akin to transparent protection against rain than to solid roofing, was developed in conjunction with Frei Otto and Fritz Leonhardt, who made a name for himself as designer of Stuttgart's filigrane television tower. The engineers applied the principle of pre-tensed cable roofs whose forms were at that time already being calculated by computer. That in conjunction with the complex technical and thermal problems facing Behnisch's team resulted in these Olympic constructions, conceived in accordance with nature, representing the age's progressive technological thinking more than any other architectural project.

Further Reading:
Die Verwirklichung einer Idee. Anlagen u. Bauten für die Olympischen Spiele 1972, Bauen + Wohnen (special issue) 1972

● An "Olympiade of short distances amid nature, the muses, and sport" was the city of Munich's objective in 1972 on an unbuilt area with the 290 m. television tower as a landmark. In the 1967 competition the Behnisch Office entered an imaginative proposal for an "Olympic landscape" transforming a neglected area into an attractive park plus lake. The idea was that the sports facilities should be embedded like hollows on the flanks of the remodelled natural area. That made the buildings seem like integrated components rather than independent architecture in a landscape which after the Games was to serve the public as a recreational area and is in fact intensively used as a park up to the present day.

The overall area with the large stadium and the various sports and training facilities constituted the most important architectural event in Germany at that time and for many years afterwards. Admiration for buildings organically adapted to the landscape and the spectacular roof design, which was viewed as a great constructional adventure, sparked off animated dis-

German Federal Parliament

Architects: Behnisch & Partners, Stuttgart
(Project Partner: Gerald Staib)
Building: New German Parliament
Location: Görresstraße, Bonn
Client: German Federal Parliament
Construction: 1987-1992

● After a prolonged planning period the German Federal Parliament's new assembly chamber was declared officially open in 1992. From the very beginning accomodation of parliamentary institutions in Bonn had been affected by lack of space. In 1949 architect Hans Schwippert adapted a college of education for utilization by the post-war German parliament but initial extensions of the buildings were necessary as early as 1956. Attempts at devising far-reaching new plans for parliament, upper chamber, and MPs' facilities were made during the sixties but came to nothing because people wanted, for political reasons, to maintain Bonn's status as a "provisional" capital. Among the public new plans were always viewed as a "betrayal" of Berlin.

Hesitation over construction of an appropriate, functional, and representative complex of parliamentary buildings also affected the development with which the Behnisch Office was involved from 1972. Over 20 years passed between Behnisch winning the competition and completion of the building. Only when at the start of the eighties people began to accept de facto the reality of two German states did the government decide in favour of a large scale "expansion of the capital". At the centre of all this planning was of course the new federal parliament. The choice of Günter Behnisch involved a man whose theorizing has for many years devoted attention to "architecture in democracy". In his work he seeks formal elements that visually embody fundamental democratic virtues. For the new parliament building at Bonn Behnisch put great emphasis on architectural implementation of the "transparency" of political processes so necessary for democracy. The parliament's great entrance hall welcomes the public. The building renounces any intimidating triumphalist architectural language. Prolonged public debates were necessary before a decision could be taken in favour of a circular plenary chamber.

The building's siting is clearly influenced by the promenade along the banks of the Rhine. Large areas of glass allow the greatest possible amount of daylight into the building. On the side facing the river the structuring of the facade is almost Japanese in its lightness.

By an irony of history, shortly after completion of this new parliament its members had to make legal provision for the modalities of moving the capital to Berlin. The contract for conversion of Berlin's old Reichstag into a new parliament went to Norman Foster, an English architect. He is faced with the difficulty of at least matching the great quality of the Bonn parliamentary building.

Further Reading:
Ingeborg Flagge, Wolfgang Jean Stock (Ed.): *Architektur in der Demokratie. Bauen für die Politik*, Stuttgart 1992

Architect: Heinz Bienefeld, Swisttal-Ollheim
Building: Haus Kühnen (conversion and extension)
Location: Willibrodstraße 19, Kevelaer
Clients: Hanna and Gert Kühnen
Construction: 1988

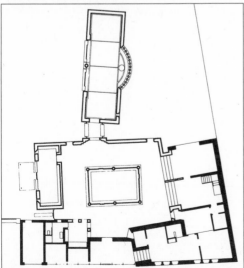

● In the work of Heinz Bienefeld (d. 1995) craftsmanship and a sense of classical mastery are particularly
apparent. His houses have been called (by W. Pehnt)
"heroic gestures of assertion of quality", emanating
the stoical calm of carefully constructed, timeless
architecture in a world of hastily thrown-together
buildings. As a loner Bienefeld has certainly succeeded
in adopting an attitude of resistance to the prevalent
Zeitgeist and thereby indicating a new way for modern architecture.

His architecture found a sufficient object in the sphere
of bourgeois dwellings. All his efforts were devoted
towards protecting that sphere and elevating it into a
place of inner contemplation. However, he did not
want to offer the architectural backdrop for any
acquiescent retreat into privacy. Despite the tranquillity emanated by the building materials, colours, and
surfaces, a tendency towards dissolution of the unified
house into its individual elements is to be felt. A liking
for the Roman house, forming a little *urbs* with its
many corridors and rooms, its inner courtyards and
fountain, endows Bienefeld's buildings with a yearning for enlivenment of the private sphere as a protective shield against a world administered by the media.
That is very beautifully embodied in the small town of
Kevelaer where a fifties corner house was to be
extended by a library and an additional living room,
known as the garden room. An atrium establishes a
link between the old and new parts of the building,
alluding to the Lower Rhine's Roman past. From this
atrium one reaches the library and garden room. The
architect broke up the overall ensemble by extending
it into the garden with each part of the building
asserting stylistic autonomy. Aesthetic coherence is,
however, assured – as in all of Bienefeld's buildings –
by the brilliance of the detail.

Further Reading:
Wilfried Wang, *Wohnhaus in Kevelaer,* in: DAM Architektur Jahrbuch 1993, pp. 62-71

Architect: Heinz Bienefeld
Building: Dwelling
Location: Brühl, Donatusstraße
Client: Roland Babanek
Construction: 1991-1996

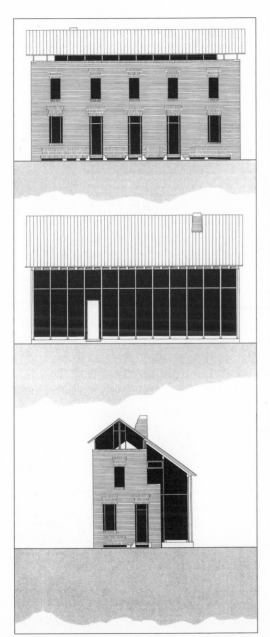

● This is one of the last houses that architect Heinz Bienefeld could complete before his death in 1995. It is a large stepped brick house with a clear-cut ground-plan. On the ground-floor of this long building is a kitchen to the right of the large entrance hall and a library to the left. On the first floor are three children's rooms and a bathroom. The parents' rooms take up the whole of the top floor. The roof is not directly supported by the walls: it is underpinned by metal pillars and thus seems to float over the building. The unusual stepped form is particularly emphasized by that construction.

On one side the roof soars asymetrically over the house's walls. Bienefeld has developed the entire house-front as a glassed-in entrance hall so that there are two facades on that side: a large glass front structured by 13 slender metal pillars, and behind that, in the vestibule area already, a second brick facade. The interior opens up by way of a diagonal, freely-floating metal staircase which ends on the first floor in a gallery-like corridor that runs the entire length of the building. From here one enters the rooms on this floor and can also overlook the entire vestibule. Another staircase, cut into the body of the building, leads to the second floor. The back of the house has the impact of a monumental wall. Inset windows create a sense of depth and endow the wall with the impressive weight of block-like stability. The house combines what seems an almost anonymous timelessness with an equally unmistakable modernity.

Two main elements in this architect's way of working are particularly apparent in this building: clarity of outlines and loving use of materials.

Further Reading:
Jan Thorn-Prikker: *Form is Everything,* in: "in" 2/1994, Inter Nationes, Bonn, pp. 24-29

Architect: Gottfried Böhm, Cologne
Building: Züblin-Haus
Location: Albstadtweg, Stuttgart
Client: Ed. Züblin AG
Construction: 1982-1984

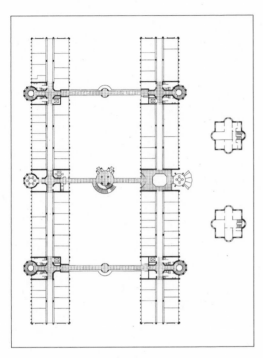

● When the Züblin construction company wanted to integrate all its branches and associated enterprises, scattered across Stuttgart, with the central administration in a single building, and sought an architect capable of designing an aesthetically appealing edifice, made from prefabricated concrete elements, for a staff of 700, it chose Gottfried Böhm. He made a name for himself as a man with great experience in using concrete. This ambitious architect, who has constantly avoided all fashionable trends, has achieved great expressivity and beauty when utilizing this material in his churches.

It is thus all the more astonishing that the most striking aspect of the Züblin-Haus is not so much the concrete facades as that part of the building which – apart from the connecting bridges and the staircase towers – seems completely incorporeal: the monumental glass hall. Glass halls are in fact a motif in many of Böhm's projects. However, only in the dimensions of the Züblin development does their significance within urban development become apparent.

On a featureless area on the outskirts of Stuttgart Böhm's "crystal palace" marked the centre of a district that does not yet exist. Between two office wings each around 100 m. long he established a 24 m. wide and 60 m. long courtyard with a glass roof, bordered on two sides by real house facades, in order to create the impression of an external area, of a "public" place.

Transparency and spaciousness are mediated by a 33 m. high hall between the office wings, completed by monumental glass walls. Nevertheless less material was used in this apparently profligate way of building than would have been needed for glassing over all the connecting bridges. Genius is also demonstrated when economy awakens an impression of luxury ...

Further Reading:
Manfred Sack, *Gottfried Böhms Züblin-Haus in Stuttgart,* in: Das Züblin-Haus, Stuttgart 1985, pp. 17-29

Architect: Gottfried Böhm, Cologne
Nikolaus Rosiny, Klaus Krüger, Lutz Rieger
Building: Saarbrücken Palace (renovation and extension)
Location: Schloßplatz, Saarbrücken
Client: Aufbaugesellschaft Saarbrücker Schloß mbH
Construction: 1982-1989

● Gottfried Böhm has gained a reputation of being master of combining the old and the new. One of the greatest challenges he has ever faced was certainly the palace at Saarbrücken where extensive restoration became necessary during the seventies. Böhm suggested that only the wings should be renovated and that the uninteresting central element should be replaced by an imposing steel and glass construction. After even traditionalists realized that discussion of reconstruction of a building that had been much changed over the course of history would be extremely prolonged, the Cologne architect was able to set to work.

The situation facing him was as follows. The triple-winged baroque palace designed by Joachim Friedrich Stengel was completed in 1748, but half the building was burnt down in 1793 during the upheavals accompanying the French Revolution. Then in 1810 Adam Knipper refashioned the palace as a classical terrace of bourgeois dwellings, one storey lower than the original. A modest new central section by Hugo Dihm was added in 1872, and the Nazis attempted to upgrade that with a neo-baroque staircase. Now this heterogeneous building – destroyed during the sec-

ond world war, patched up again in makeshift fashion, and increasingly dilapidated as the years passed – was once again to be made into Saarbrücken's "crowning feature".

Böhm conceived the towering new central projection as something eye-catching. This brings together old and new elements in the building, and on the garden side visibly rests on the remains of Dihm's golden sandstone facade. The new construction, standing proudly between palace wings painted a restrained greyish white, is reminiscent of 19th century greenhouse architecture. Its character changes in accordance with the time of day or year. A dark sky transforms it into a gloomy fortress and bright sunshine into a cheerful pavilion akin with its mansard roof to French precursors. Inside attention is particularly attracted by the upper hall, used for functions and concerts, where Böhm in person embellished the ceiling with abstract perspectival painting, deploying spray technique with great precision. That was done as a reflection of the palace's baroque origins – and certainly also to satisfy the architect's own inclination towards creating a *Gesamtkunstwerk,* an all-embracing work of art.

Further Reading:
Werner Strodthof, *Neue Stadtkrone. Gottfried Böhm und das Schloß in Saarbrücken,* in: Bauwelt 21/1989, p. 96/97

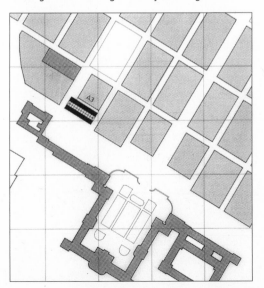

Architects: Hans-Busso von Busse, Heinz Blees, Roland Büch,
Niels Kampmann, Munich
Building: Arrivals and departures area: Terminal 1, central building
with tower, multi-storey car parks, external facilities, city rail-link
Location: Munich II Airport
Client: Flughafen München GmbH
Construction: 1987-1992

Hans-Busso von Busse

● The search around Munich for a site for the city's new airport, capable of coping with 20 million passagers annually, took six years, but Erdinger Moos finally seemed to be the right place. After a two-stage competition, where Busse & Partners emerged as winners, detailed planning got under way in 1978 in the hope that the new airport could be opened in 1985. However, action by conservationists and other opponents of the airport led in 1981 to imposition of an injunction against construction. That was only overturned by the Administrative Court four years later. Despite that disruption and intervening changes to essential aspects of the programme, an exemplary – in aesthetic, functional, and cybernetic terms – passenger check-in area was inaugurated in May 1992.

The architects' prime intention was to develop a highly efficient system for complex movements and transportation processes based on the most modern technology, thereby devising a group of buildings that both fit into the landscape and fulfil passengers' needs for orientation and well-being. To achieve this, the integration of light and its many possibilities of determining the character and atmosphere of spaces was declared to be the plan's overall theme. However, in order to avoid destroying light's modulatory richness with shrieking colours, the architects decided to construct a "white airport". This lies beneath the extended skies of a landscape with straight paths, alleys, ditches, and dykes. That "geometry" influenced the lay-out of the extended airport buildings whose height was determined by surrounding trees and the lines of the horizon.

The open structure of this spatial concept is captivating. It testifies to a discriminating approach to planning, and at the same time makes an essential contribution to orientation. The architects' interpretation of functionality is that passengers should feel at ease and find their way in a big building without difficulty.

Further Reading:
Werkbericht 2 – Flughafen München, published by the Institut für internationale Architektur-Dokumentation, Munich 1993

Architects: Erick van Egeraat associated architects, Rotterdam
Building: Multiple dwelling
Location: Störzbachstraße, Stuttgart
Client: LEG Landesentwicklungsgesellschaft Baden-Württemberg,
Stuttgart
Construction: 1993

Erick van Egeraat

51

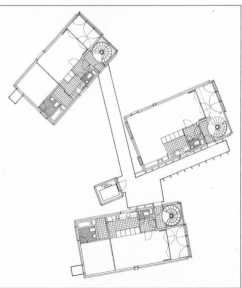

● House No. 13, erected as part of the International Garden Exhibition, is not in fact a house but rather consists of three residential towers linked horizontally by a pergola system and vertically by a glass lift tower. In addition each building has its own stairwell whose spiral steps can take on a public or a private character, depending on whether individual storeys constitute self-contained dwellings, maisonettes, or even large apartments involving three or more floors. Each flat consists of a "loft" (a large room that can be divided up as required) and a service zone providing a hallway, WC, kitchen, and bathroom. All these dwellings face south. On the outside are small conservatories so as to make the most of the sunlight and to reduce street-noise. Everyone living here can reach the roof-terrace on the middle house by way of the lift and pergola. Inhabitants can pursue joint activities here and in the gardens between the residential towers.

It is not just chance that these original buildings were devised by a Dutch architect. A well-established tradition both takes into account changing needs with regard to housing and meets high standards of aesthetic design. This plan is convincing overall with its dissolution of the apartment block into three excitingly related towers, and also pleases with the structuring of the extensively glassed facades facing the sun.

Further Reading:
Mecanoo, *Mehrfamilienhaus in Stuttgart,* DAM Architektur Jahrbuch 1994, pp. 130-135

Five Terrace Houses

Architects: Eisele + Fritz, Darmstadt
Building: Five terrace houses
Location: Heinrich-Delp-Straße, Darmstadt-Eberstadt
Client: Bauverein für Arbeiterwohnungen Darmstadt
Construction: 1992-1993

● It was for the Workers Housing Association that Johann Eisele and Nicolas Fritz planned five terrace houses right next to a primary school in the south of Darmstadt. After the architects had analyzed the terrace house as unifying aspects of community and individuality, they adhered faithfully to the slogan that the essence of architecture entails uncovering the principles involved in any task. The front, west, and east sides of this terrace were given a smoothly-plastered facade with just small openings, and trellis-work runs the length of the construction, creating the impression of a unified building. The south-facing garden side of each of the five houses appears as a separate unit – in the justifiable expectation that individualization would be continued in the different ways inhabitants organized their gardens.

These terrace houses will certainly be recognized by their roofs, which stab like saw-teeth into the sky as if they had just been opened up. Such a striking gesture characterizes the provisional aspect and delight in experimentation of an architecture which views the planning process as a voyage of discovery through the multiple possibilities of finding adequate and at the same time surprisingly unconventional solutions to the problems involved.

Further Reading:
Sägezahn. Reihenhäuser in Darmstadt, in: AIT Architektur-Innenarchitektur 1-2/1994, pp. 50-53

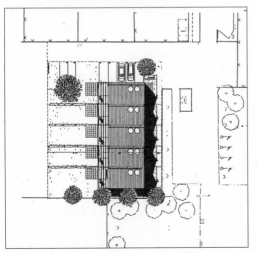

Architects: Sir Norman Foster and Partners, London
Building: Haus der Wirtschaftsförderung
Location: Mülheimer Straße 100, Duisburg
Client: Kaiser Bautechnik, Duisburg
Construction: 1989-1991

● In the heart of the Ruhr, between Duisburg and Dortmund, there is a densely settled and much polluted industrial landscape which is in particular danger of falling behind future social and economic developments. That is why the Emscher-Park International Building Exhibition was established, providing the region with forward-looking impulses in the realms of ecology, economics, technology, house-building, and culture. Instead of mines and the iron and steel industry high-tech and service enterprises increasingly shape the new image of the Ruhr. In Duisburg this structural change is exemplarily presented in the development of a micro-electronics park that is dominated by three buildings, all devised by Norman Foster: the House for the Promotion of Industry and Commerce, the Technology Centre III, and the glass hall of the Micro-Electronics Centre where modern commercial and office facilities are intended to further the opening of new enterprises.

The first to be built was the House for the Promotion of Industry and Commerce whose architecture alone – even when seen from afar – presents the process of modernization it is hoped will take place in the micro-electronics park. On a relatively small site Foster has succeeded in establishing a building whose dynamic elegance makes an architectural virtue of confine-

ment. An elegant ocean liner of steel and glass has dropped anchor on the much-used Mülheimer Straße. Highly modern technology prevails inside the building. A single control-unit optimizes thermal conditions in each office, and also allows individual corrections of temperature and of the amount of light and warmth permeating the transparent facade. Warmed or cooled air from outside is supplied without noise, and surplus heat is removed from rooms by way of radiation-exchange utilizing water-permeated cooling-ceilings. Foster's office has many years of experience with innovative technology in such large-scale projects as the Hong Kong and Shanghai Bank and Tokyo's Century Tower. In Germany his firm will become known to the general public through its involvement in reconstructing the Reichstag to accomodate the new German parliament, a project that got under way in 1995.

Further Reading:
Peter Rumpf, *Geometrie und Technologie,* in: Bauwelt 19/1993, pp. 1002-1014

Architect: Frank O. Gehry, Santa Monica (USA)
Planning: Günter Pfeifer, Lörrach
Building: Design Museum
Location: Vitra company area, Weil am Rhein
Client: Vitra GmbH
Construction: 1988-1989

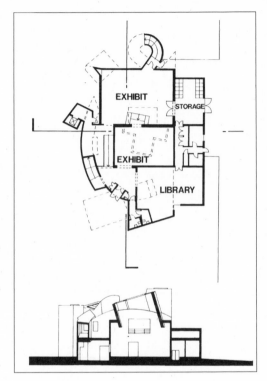

● Frank O. Gehry's constructions are solitaries which are more likely to relate to the landscape than to surrounding buildings; they are always developed from within, from out of their intimacy. Their remarkable bulgings are all motivated by the particular nature of the inner rooms and a striving towards daylight, which enters by way of bizarre cuboids serving as light-shafts. Room by room his architecture grows outwards, thereby gaining a heterogeneous structure composed of a great variety of architectural elements that seem to entail an accumulation of several smaller buildings – an urban backdrop imposed on top of the light-filled intimate rooms.

The Design Museum at Weil am Rhein appears absolutely cave-like with its modest exhibition area of 740 sq. m. It is tiny alongside Gehry's factory (10,000 sq. m.) completed at the same time. However, the architect had other connections in mind, far removed from the profane industrial buildings in the immediate vicinity. He sees his museum in artistic and geographical conjunction with Le Corbusier's expressively structured pilgrimage church at Ronchamp on the south slope of the Vosges, and with Rudolf Steiner's spiritually organic Goetheanum at Dornach in Switzerland. Unlike those serious buildings, the Design Museum does not lack irony. It leaves a slight impression of having been "thrown together" as if an anarchistic spirit had wanted to demonstrate the art of architectural improvisation.

Further Reading:
Paulgerd Jesberg, *Das Vitra-Design-Museum von Frank O. Gehry,* in: Baukultur 1/1990, pp. 22-25

Architects: von Gerkan, Marg & Partners, Hamburg
Planning: Meinhard von Gerkan with Karsten Brauer
Building: Passenger Terminal
Location: Hamburg Fuhlsbüttel Airport
Client: Flughafen Hamburg GmbH
Construction: 1990-1993

Meinhard von Gerkan

● Hamburg's old airport had to be extended and modernized as quickly as possible after plans for a big new development outside the city had fallen through. While flights continued it was possible to build a new passenger terminal on the basis of a plan that provides for renovation of the airport in several stages. With Meinhard von Gerkan's project, offering an elegant arrivals and departures hall, the north-south pier with aircraft bays, and a cylindrical car park, this Hanseatic city has established the basis for a modern airport.

The new plan yields a possibility of successively replacing the somewhat timid fifties architecture which has dominated the scene to date. New terminals can be attached to the pier that constitutes the backbone of these proposals. The core of the old facilities, the brick reception building dating from 1928, can, however, be saved. The plans leave space for this monument to the pioneering days of civil aviation, which the architects would like to be used as a museum. The new terminal building is a spacious, well-lit hall, almost as big as a football pitch. Passengers arriving and departing will be dealt with on two storeys with those who have just landed channelled through the lower floor. The large departures area offers shops, restaurants, and visitor facilities at different levels beneath the mighty 39 m. high floating roof. With a span of 62 m. it rests on seven triangular steel truss beams, carried by twelve concrete pillars with shaped stanchions. High windows provide the desired quality of daylight for the hall so that the uncovered steel construction can be clearly seen against the light. The roof structure was inspired by an aeroplane wing viewed in profile. Its dynamically curved form is counterpointed on two sides by seemingly monolithic, block-like segments of buildings with square window patterns – behind which offices are accomodated on several floors.

Further Reading:
Flughafen Hamburg, Passagierterminal, in: Centrum Jahrbuch für Architektur und Stadt 1994, pp. 174-179
Fuhlsbüttel Airport, in: Meinhard von Gerkan, Architecture for Transportation, Birkhäuser Verlag Basel 1997, pp. 88–106

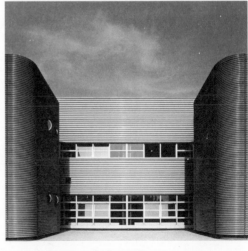

Architects: Nicholas Grimshaw & Partners, London
Building: Production and administrative building
Location: Vitra company area, Weil am Rhein
Client: Vitra GmbH
Construction: 1981

● Industrial building remains a neglected area of architecture, usually leading a wretched existence in the care of engineers. Subjugated to extreme demands for economic viability, unaffected by aesthetic ambitions, and largely unified by way of standardized forms of construction, industrial architecture normally involves endless variations on "boxes". On the other hand, it should not be forgotten that decisive impulses within the development of modern architecture have time and again come from engineering and industrial construction.

It is absolutely clear that architects like Nicholas Grimshaw – whose architecture includes many industrial buildings – uphold modernist aesthetics and wish to advance the dialectic between form and function as the crucial aspect of architectural design. This process is furthered by involvement in difficult tasks and by rapidly developing constructional technology which constantly makes new solutions possible. That was also the case with the Vitra production hall replacing a burnt-out building, which had to be ready within just six months to meet insurance requirements. This hall has 6 m. headroom, a production area of 9,500 sq. m., and an additional 2,500 sq. m. for office and exhibition rooms. To allow production to start again in January 1982 the architect chose a twin-shell con-

struction using sheet-steel units. The hall could thus be in full use while the outer skin was still being assembled.

A standardized, prefabricated reinforced concrete skeleton spanning 25 m. was used for the support system. All the installations are visible beneath the roof and along the outer walls. The six square towers added on to the building, housing staff washrooms and rest areas, are a significant aspect of the hall's form. These "satellites", which are painted blue, also serve to enliven the 125 m. long facades of powder-coated aluminium.

Further Reading:
Schnelle Kiste. Stuhlproduktion und Verwaltung in Weil am Rhein, in: DBZ 12/1983, pp. 30/31

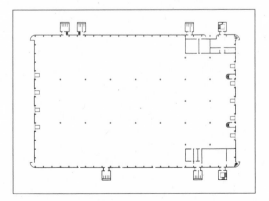

Architect: Walter Gropius
Replanning: Alex Cvijanovic, Hans Bandel
Building: Bauhaus Archive, Museum of Design
Location: Klingelhöferstraße 14, Berlin
Client: Senator für Bau- u. Wohnungswesen
Construction: 1976-1978

● In 1960 the man who established the Bauhaus archive, Hans M. Wingler, found an initial home for it at Darmstadt, consisting of just two rooms. The idea was that this provisional set-up should be replaced by a new institute whose implementation Wingler began to plan. In January 1964 he wrote to Gropius that the Darmstadt city authorities would assist construction of an archive building as soon as a leading architect had produced an outline design. Darmstadt's Rosenhöhe was the favoured site. Just a few months later Gropius produced a plan that already proposed the characteristic clerestory roofs with their high windows for lighting rooms. However, the Darmstadt authorities saw no way of financing this project, estimated at 4.5 million DM. In 1968 Wingler and Gropius were in Berlin together and the idea of establishing the archive there was born. Gropius died before he could adapt his plans to the new site along the Landwehrkanal, so his colleague Alex Cvijanovic assumed responsibility for implementing the Darmstadt plan as faithfully as possible. Nevertheless the new location compelled two major alterations. Gropius's ideas about the access system had to be modified and the light-scoops made higher so as to prevent the building seeming too small on a sloping area. The Archive thus gained a striking outline but the internal proportions of the exhibition rooms were changed. The revised plan was ready in 1972, but by then not much remained of Gropius's original design. The Landwehrkanal building combined the influences of Gropius, Cvijanovic, and Hans Bandel who implemented the project. Yet Berlin can maintain that it possesses imposing cultural monuments by three of its great sons: the Nationalgalerie by Mies van der Rohe, Hans Scharoun's Philharmonie, and the Bauhaus-Archiv by Walter Gropius.

Further Reading:
Christian Wolsdorff, *Ein Entwurf in eigener Sache,* in: Von der Idee zum Werk (catalogue), Bonn 1991

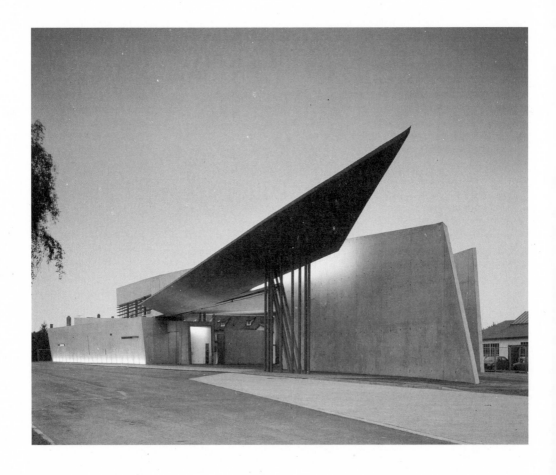

Architect: Zaha M. Hadid, London
Planning: Günter Pfeifer & Roland Mayer, Lörrach
Building: Fire brigade building
Location: Vitra company area, Weil am Rhein
Client: Vitra GmbH
Construction: 1992-1993

● Few women have achieved prominence on the international architectural scene. Outstanding personalities such as Gae Aulenti from Milan are for the moment exceptions. Nonetheless if one contemplates the small group of people belonging to today's architectural avantgarde, in their midst is Zaha M. Hadid, born at Baghdad in 1950. This Iraqui is certainly an exceptional talent. At 21 she concluded a mathematics course in her home city and went to London to study with Rem Kohlhaas at the celebrated Architectural Association. In 1977 she opened her own office in London and, aged just 32, achieved an international breakthrough with her spectacular design for Hong Kong's "Peak Club" where she came out on top against over 600 competitors.

This project gave exemplary expression to the fact that its architect views herself as being in the tradition of Futurism and Russian Constructivism, which she combines with the possibilities offered by rapid technological progress so as at long last to achieve implementation of an utopian dream dating from the twenties. One has to learn to see anew in order to understand the superimposed perspectives of Zaha Hadid's plans, immersed in acrylic colours and cool gloss paints, where areas are derestricted and dissected, walls, floors, and roofs burst apart, and there arises an impression of weightlessness. Like interstellar flotsam and jetsam architectural components fly past those fearlessly contemplating these plans. And yet all that is supposed to be implementable. Zaha Hadid

pushed ahead her Hong Kong plan in hundreds of detailed drawings up to the point of readiness for construction, but then her client withdrew from the project because of the city's uncertain political future. Nevertheless during the past few years a number of smaller-scale plans have been realized. They include the building for the company fire brigade on the Vitra site. The idea of red fire-fighting appliances racing with howling sirens across the company area, against the backdrop of flickering lights and a blazing furniture factory, of course had to arouse the enthusiasm of an architect who views herself as implementing Futurism. The outcome is a building where movement has petrified. This expresses the tension of being on the alert and the dormant power of a fire brigade team that at any moment can explode into action.

Further Reading:
Das Feuerwehrhaus in Weil am Rhein, in: DBZ 7/1993, pp. 1129-1134

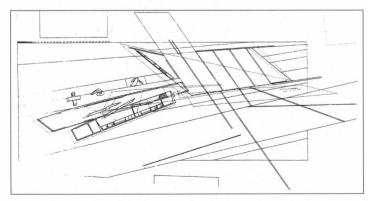

Architect: Herman Hertzberger, Amsterdam
Building: Residential block with inner courtyard
Location: Lindenstraße, Berlin
Client: IBA Berlin
Construction: 1984-1986

● The Netherlands has a long tradition of construction of modern housing and settlements, broken only by the second world war. Dutch architects have upheld the idea that housing requires a friendly and easily comprehensible environment which provides users with great freedom of movement and possibilities of contact. They were thus somewhat sceptical about the one-sidedly analytical character of the "Charter of Athens", that most celebrated manifesto of modern planning presenting the city as a primitive, schematically manufacturable machine.

The search for alternative planning models found its Dutch mouthpiece in "Forum", a journal published since 1959 by architects Aldo van Eyck, Jacob Berend Bakema, and Herman Hertzberger. This editorial cooperation led to "Dutch Structuralism", which was interpreted in many different ways. As an architect Hertzberger has primarily been concerned with providing an architectural framework – rather than ready-made living and working environments – which users can then fill out in accordance with personal inclinations. He has produced housing that convincingly promotes interaction between individual and community, and private and public spheres. The Dutch architect presented the concept of a "housing chain",

grouping flats and communal stairways devised as semi-open communication areas, in a contribution to "documenta urbana" at Kassel. Shortly afterwards for the Berlin IBA he devised another "housing chain" showing it is possible to orient sufficiently-lit dwellings towards an inner courtyard with an inviting garden accessible to the public. That is achieved by way of stairways with open means of access – a house without house-doors. Apart from the courtyard the roof-garden also serves as a communal area. A differentiated approach to transition from the private sphere of the flats to the public realm characterizes a way of building whose aesthetic ambitions are always directly derived from its social objectives.

Further Reading:
Woningencomplex, in: Wessel Reinink (Ed.), Herman Hertzberger, Architekt, Amsterdam 1990, pp. 76-79

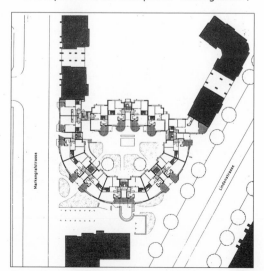

Architect: Herzog + Partners, Munich
Assistant: Peter Bonfig
Building: Youth education centre hostel
Location: Windberg, Lower Bavaria
Client: Kloster Windberg
Construction: 1987-1990

● Most artistically ambitious architects scorn ecological thinking. Aesthetics and protection of the environment seem to be contradictions. Thomas Herzog represents an opposing viewpoint. With his buildings he time and again demonstrates that a highly ambitious and idiosyncratic structure can be combined with energy-saving technology.

At Windberg, a small town in the south of the Bayerischer Wald, a dormitory hostel for around 100 young guests was to be built in close proximity to an old monastery, which houses a youth education centre, and the immediate surroundings newly landscaped. In his plan the architect was, on the one hand, inspired by the built environment – the long monastery walls, the nearby church tower, and the big wooden village barns – , while, on the other, interesting ideas about energy-saving determined the structure of the new hostel.

The length of the building was divided into two zones. In the wider southern part are the dormitories, little used by day but constantly by night. The southern facade was thus constructed completely anew as a "heating wall", which warms up by day and releases the stored heat inwards by night. That process is backed during the winter months by a gas-powered heating system where small radiators are sufficient in the south-facing rooms. In the summer a large projecting roof and external venetian blinds provide protection against too much sun and over-heating.

The narrower northern part of the building, devised as a skeletal wooden construction, houses washing and storage facilities. Those are sited here because they are only used for short periods and require minimal heating. The warm water for showers comes from six large tanks which are heated by way of pipe-collectors on the southern roof. A display-board in the entrance area explains this energy-system to guests, showing changes in temperature digitally.

Further Reading:
Neubauten der Prämonstratenser-Abtei in Windberg, in: DAM Jahrbuch für Architektur 1991, pp. 166-171

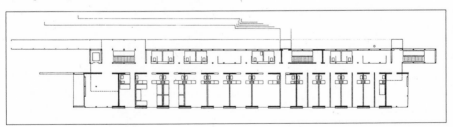

Architect: Herzog + Partners, Munich
Landscaping: Anneliese and Peter Latz
Building: Production halls and energy centre
Location: Landerfeld 8, Eimbeckhausen
Client: Wilkhahn
Construction: 1989-1992

● The Wilkhahn company is not just oriented towards modernity in aesthetic terms. It has also taken on the responsibility of ensuring that its production methods constantly reflect social and, increasingly, ecological considerations. Company architecture is charged with supporting that process, making improvement of the working world its main task. Special significance is attached to overall structuring of the entire company area, both buildings and open land. The firm thus had a general plan drawn up to provide a framework for further expansion. Thomas Herzog was charged with implementing that and has already developed a large structure housing production halls and an energy centre.

The main impact exerted by the new production halls is by way of the upper floor, executed as a modern wide-span wooden construction. This is punctuated by four idiosyncratically designed vertical elements. Between those hang the pillar-free hall roofs, covered with greenery which provides protection against summer heat, reduces noise emissions, delays rain flow-off, and provides compensation for the land lost to building. The rainwater from roofs and courtyards is directed to a new pond area. There is thus always sufficient water available for fire-fighting so that local supplies do not have to be used. On the completely shadow-free south side the projecting roofs are equipped with a photo-voltaic installation for producing energy. Heating utilizes a roof radiation system, and is regulated in accordance with the weather and time of day.

Further Reading:
Kulturlandschaft. Produktionshallen der Firma Wilkhahn, in: db deutsche bauzeitung 2/1994, pp. 14-20

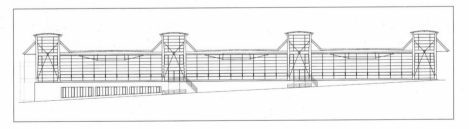

Architects: Herzog & de Meuron, Basel
Building: House for a collection of contemporary art
Location: Oberföhringerstraße 103, Munich
Client: Ingvild Goetz
Construction: 1991-1992

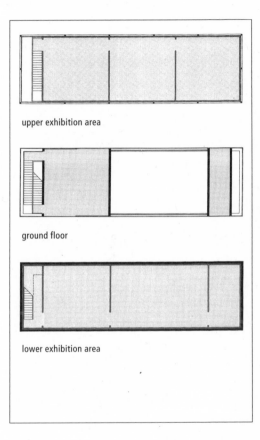

upper exhibition area

ground floor

lower exhibition area

● A private client in Munich has shown that an exemplary gallery building can be erected on just a small budget. This will do complete justice to its task of adequate presentation of a collection of contemporary art (with works by Nauman, Twombly, Kounellis, Rückriem, etc) and can also be viewed as a mini architectural "manifesto", resulting from the architects' conceptual treatment of light. Jacques Herzog and Pierre de Meuron have completely fulfilled – at the highest architectural level – the demand that a museum should be a building with four walls and light from above.

The building's wonderful use of materials contributes to both the surprising spaciousness of the rooms and the thought-provoking availability of light from above even on the cellar level. Here – if not previously – one becomes aware that the building's external symmetry does not reveal all the secrets of what seems such a simple construction. In reality the gallery consists of a 24 m. long and 8 m. wide wooden structure sitting on an equally large configuration of concrete. The latter is half sunk into the ground so that only the upper completely glazed part is visible. A similar strip of opaque glass also completes the upper wooden part of the gallery. In both cases the glass allows dazzle-free light to enter the exhibition rooms. On the upper floor three rooms are lit in that way, while on the lower level one utilizes daylight and another lower room artificial light. That is made possible by a small ground-level intermediate floor incorporating the entrance. From there the astonished visitor reaches rooms whose quality of lighting is scarcely equalled by any of our big museums.

Further Reading:
Haus für eine zeitgenössische Kunstsammlung, in: DAM Architektur Jahrbuch 1993, pp. 103-109

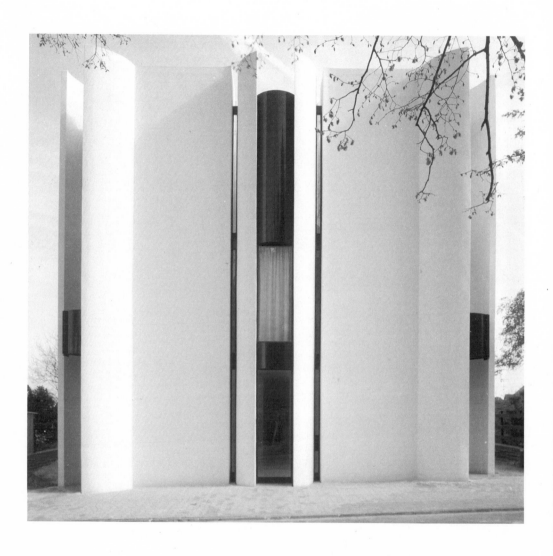

Architect: Johannes Peter Hölzinger, Bad Nauheim
Building: Residential building
Location: Gustav-Kayser-Straße 4, Bad Nauheim
Client: The architect
Construction: 1975-1977

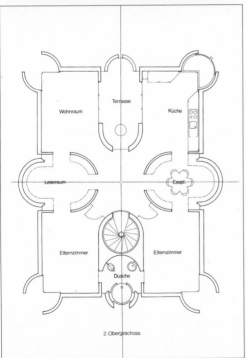

● Johannes Peter Hölzinger bridges disciplines and does not accept Adolf Loos's energetically propagated difference between architecture and art. However, unlike many "artist-architects", he has dedicated himself to an avantgarde concept of art implemented in everyday practice. On the one hand, awareness of unfamiliar aesthetic experiences is sensitized by way of his architecture, which makes great demands on inhabitants' sensuous perception, while, on the other, the aesthetic element ultimately becomes a daily experience through the necessity of utilizing this artistically-shaped architecture as a living-space.
Even though the white screen-walls do not seem to form a unified architectural construction, this residence stands like a fortress protecting an avantgarde feeling towards life amid a row of Gründerzeit houses from the late nineteenth century. Some structural characteristics of the surrounding buildings were taken over as organizational elements, but the diagonal alignment of the windows in Hölzinger's creation, providing an open view past the neighbouring villas, shows that contact is not sought with the other houses and their inhabitants. Despite the closed exterior an astonishing abundance of light exists on the first floor already, and at the higher level, with its Mediterranean-style inner terrace and lighting from above, this seems to explode.

Further Reading:
Paulgerd Jesberg, *Integration von Kunst und Architektur,* in: DBZ 11/1993, pp. 1837-1849

Architect: Hans Hollein, Vienna
Building: Städtisches Museum Abteiberg
Location: Abteistraße 27, Mönchengladbach
Client: Stadt Mönchengladbach
Construction: 1976-1982

● Hans Hollein's design for the Abteiberg launched a considerable number of museum buildings intended to be more than just protective shells for valuable exhibition objects. After long decades of programmatically prescribed functionality, a new generation of architects undertook an attempt at once again ennobling architecture as art. In Mönchengladbach Hollein was concerned with creative confrontation between the aesthetic autonomy of the works of art on show and his architecture's claims to being art.

Over the course of time the museum's first director, Johannes Cladders, had assembled an internationally celebrated collection of modern art at Mönchengladbach. That gave rise to the wish to create an appropriate architectural setting for this collection. From the start Hollein's new building was conceived as a component in an ensemble of educational institutions, which were gradually to be established

on the Abteiberg. With its art museum Mönchengladbach wanted to institute a form of adult education that was integrated in urban cultural life. The architect thus had his museum built into the hillside so that its roofs could be walked on as a public forum and used in a multitude of ways. Instead of a forbiddingly solitary edifice he devised an inviting, spatially-sculpted, architectural landscape, only broken by the tower of the administrative block and some superstructure conveying light from the north to subterranean exhibition rooms.

A little marble temple serves as entrance to the underworld of the museum, which is structured in terms of individual rooms, space for changing exhibitions, and a flexibly subdividable area for the permanent collection. The organization of the whole follows the idea of a "walking through" inspired by curiosity rather than the principle of linear order. Hollein wanted to create a living museum, inviting visitors to spend time there by way of a diversity of spatial experiences.

Further Reading:
Wolfgang Pehnt, *Der Anfang der Bescheidenheit,* Munich 1983, pp. 235-240

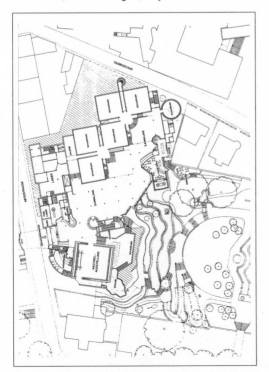

Architect: Toyo Ito, Tokyo
Site management: Scheffler & Warschauer, Frankfurt a. M.
Building: Day nursery, Eckenheim
Location: Sigmund-Freud-Straße, Frankfurt a. M.
Client: Stadt Frankfurt am Main
Construction: 1990-1991

● In 1985 the city of Frankfurt launched a remarkable programme, envisaging the building of over thirty day nurseries in different parts of the city so as to meet mounting demand for infant care. In addition the authorities wanted to apply to different districts the planning methods utilized for the museum quarter along the river Main where high-quality architecture promoted the city's image.

Both well-known German architects and international offices were commissioned to produce plans. In recent years kindergartens have been designed here by the Bolles-Wilson German-Australian team, by Viennese artist Friedensreich Hundertwasser, Hans Kollhoff, Christoph Mäckler, and many others. However, what started so ambitiously ten years ago must now give way to a cost-cutting modular construction system developed by Frankfurt's department of structural engineering. The city's money has run out and that puts an end to ambitious kindergarten architecture. Among the architects called in from abroad was Toyo Ito from Japan, who contributed one of the most remarkable plans. Amid a typical seventies housing

development Ito's kindergarten constitutes a "happy island" despite inhospitable surroundings. This is a long, curving single-storey building whose gently rising north side is covered with earth and plants. Towards the south-west the nursery opens up to the sun and the playground where there is a wooden tower and activities rooms. Three "little temples", used for homework areas, rise curiously above the earth wall. The lens-shaped roof thus sits on the completely buried multi-function room as if a UFO had landed there. Beneath this roof, however, is not any high-tech control room but rather a cave-like space without corners or edges, lit from above by a porthole. Ito's imaginative architecture aims at offering security and openness to children who for the most part have to live with their families in rented accomodation that is much too cramped and confining.

Further Reading:
Christof Bodenbach: *Kindertagesstätte in Frankfurt-Eckenheim,* in: DBZ 2/1995, pp. 59-66

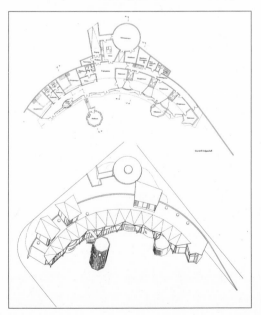

Architect: Barbara Jakubeit, Darmstadt
Planning: Staatliches Hochbauamt 1 Karlsruhe
Building: Reconstruction of Schloß Gottesaue
Location: Wollfahrtsweierer-Straße, Karlsruhe
Client: Land Baden-Württemberg
Construction: 1982-1989

● In the seventies when modern urban planning, which had made a stand against the old city and its architecture, was attacked as being destructive and anti-culture, and when the concept of conservation gained ground, attempts were made everywhere to lavishly restore and save the last remaining buildings from former times – even when, as with Schloß Gottesaue, they were in ruins. Of course serious problems had to be faced here. Reliable plans, appropriate building materials, and craft know-how were seldom available. In addition, these old buildings usually had to be put to a new use, necessitating complete reorganization of the original spatial structure and development. Conservationists sometimes despaired over such a situation, while architects were attracted by the challenge of staging an exciting dialogue between old and new, tradition and modernity.

That was also the case with Schloß Gottesaue, left in ruins after being devastated by fire in world war two, where Barbara Jakubeit had the task of rebuilding the castle, taking into account its history, while transforming this edifice into a modern college of music with concert and lecture halls, practice rooms, and library. But what original state should serve as a model for the reconstructed Gottesaue: the Renaissance residence built in the late 16th century for the Margrave of Baden-Durlach, or its early 18th century successor, reduced by one floor and given a Baroque appearance? Since the planned college took up considerable space a decision was taken in favour of reconstruction of the Renaissance castle as a starting-point, but the architect insisted that only the facade should retain its historical appearance while what had been destroyed for ever – the interior, the roof, and the windows – should be recreated in modern terms.

The new multi-layered metal windows, the lead sheeting on the steep roof with its stylized dormers, and the ridge-level fanlighting do endow the building with a contemporary character. That is continued inside in the steel used for staircases and galleries, the coffered ceilings, and of course the restructuring of the top floor with its pointed gables. This top storey houses the library, a "fascinating, crystalline room" circumscribed by a filigrane steel construction – in the words of the eulogy accompanying presentation of the Hugo Häring Prize to the architect in 1991.

Further Reading:
Wiederaufbau von Schloß Gottesaue, in: DAM Jahrbuch für Architektur 1991, pp. 142-155

Architects: Jochem Jourdan, Bernhard Müller, Sven Albrecht,
Norbert Berghof, Michael Landes, Wolfgang Rang,
Frankfurt a. M.
Building: Land Central Bank
Location: Taunusplatz, Frankfurt a. M.
Client: Landeszentralbank
Construction: 1984-1987

● Frankfurt am Main is the only city in the Federal Republic whose skyline is formed of high-rise buildings and constantly changing. At present a heaven-storming giant is once again being constructed there, Europe's highest office block at just under 260 m. This was commissioned by the Commerzbank which will for a short time thus stand above all competition until overshadowed by an even higher bank tower. Engineering technology keeps pace with such skyscrapers whilst architecture has long fallen by the wayside in the competition for the highest building.

Hesse's Central Bank took that situation into account and wanted its new building to be a horizontal structure fitting in with the city. To prevent this edifice repeating the vices of a modernism that has degenerated into glass boxes, the bank commissioned designs from two Frankfurt architectural offices which are among the most creative German champions of stylish urban post-modernism. As anticipated, the architects took into account the surrounding buildings, particularly two listed structures: a pompous Gründerzeit villa and the main building of the former Reichsbank dating from the early thirties. Neither of them are encroached on by the monumental new edifice, and in fact the distance between these buildings allowed for a little urban stone square. The coming into being of urban spaces is in fact the declared objective of a plan aiming at establishment of a modest city backdrop. The new building is 70 m. wide and 120 m. long. With four floors it picks up the eaves level of nearby 19th century buildings and continues the spatial aspect of street-long building with a comb-like perimeter block alleviated by interspersed office tracts and inner courtyards as if it were a complex of buildings with several houses. The shared backbone involves a glass-roofed hall, encouraging meetings and relaxation, inspired by 19th century arcades.

Further Reading:
Jochem Jourdan, *Die Landeszentralbank in Frankfurt am Main*, in: DAM Jahrbuch für Architektur 1989, pp. 175-192

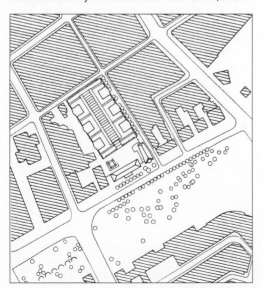

Architects: Kiessler + Partners, Munich
Building: Rhine-Elbe Science Park
Location: Bochumer Straße, Gelsenkirchen
Client: Land Nordrhein-Westfalen
Construction: 1992-1995

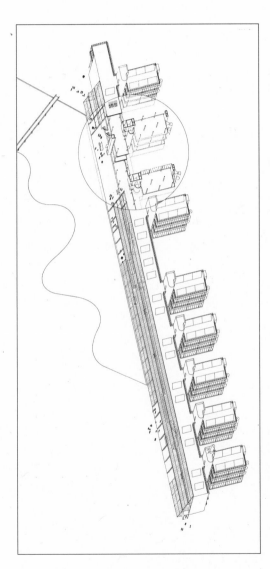

● The falling into disuse of large inner-city industrial sites is characteristic of the Ruhr. That is the outcome of the region's immense economic problems, caused by the rapid decline in jobs in manufacturing industry. The area now covered by the Rhine-Elbe Science Park became available when an old cast-steel works was pulled down. That enterprise is to be replaced by future-oriented research institutes, generously planned on the seven hectare site. Uwe Kiessler hit on the idea of making the area into a park, shielding it from the road with a long building which will be adorned with one of the world's largest, roof-installed solar power stations. The ground-plan of this architectural complex consists of three elements: the narrow three-storey tract housing the institutes, the adjacent 10 m. wide and 300 m. long arcade with a sloping glass facade, and a chain of similarly-sized three-storey pavilions.

Of course the arcade, fronting an artificial lake, is the building's most eye-catching feature. It is conceived as a public boulevard, intended to prevent the science and research lodged in the pavilion buildings from leading an isolated existence. In the summer the entire length of the glass facade's lower elements can be mechanically raised so that the boulevard opens up to the lake and becomes usable as a sun terrace. With this arcade, which is supposed to be filled with all kinds of shops, book-stores, bistros, and restaurants, the architect has created a possibility of this building, one of the showpiece attractions of the IBA Emscher Park, becoming an enticement for both those who work there and people living nearby. For that achievement he received the 1995 German Architecture Prize.

Further Reading:
Wissenschaftspark Gelsenkirchen, in: Bauwelt 9/1995, pp. 424-433

Architect: Josef Paul Kleihues, Berlin
Building: Henniger Museum and Municipal Gallery
Location: Stuttgarter Straße 93, Kornwestheim
Client: Stadt Kornwestheim
Construction: 1988-1989

● Josef Paul Kleihues is among the astonishingly few architects for whom practice and theoretical reflection are inseparably linked. His work is oriented towards the Rational Architecture established by Italian-born Aldo Rossi, enriched with technological and classical formal elements, in an attempt to find a way out of exhausted modernism to an architectural language of its own. For these "Rationalists" the ordering structure of the city is an important point of reference, which they endeavour to interpret in their plans. In his concept for a municipal gallery at Kornwestheim (to the north of Stuttgart) Kleihues also responded to the pre-existing town layout. The building's form was chosen so as to reflect and harmonize with various streets, buildings, and squares.

The gallery has two levels of exhibition areas. On the ground floor is the space for changing exhibitions, which is equipped with movable walls and receives light from above by way of a diagonally-installed strip of windows in the east facade. The permanent collection is on the second floor, supplied with light from the north through roof windows. Characteristic of Kleihues is the facade cladding where beautiful natural stone (travertine) contrasts with the "technological" roofs.

Further Reading:
Die Städtische Galerie Kornwestheim, in: Detail 4/1991, pp. 374-378

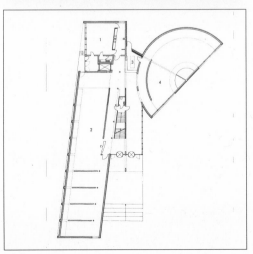

Architect: Josef Paul Kleihues, Berlin
Building: "Kant Triangle" Office Building
Location: Corner of Kantstraße/Fasanenstraße, Berlin
Client: KapHag Unternehmungsgruppe
Construction: 1992-1995

● In Berlin Josef Paul Kleihues has several times demonstrated that the city's architecture must be determined by architects if it is not to degenerate into the uninspired reflection of an indecisive planning bureaucracy or nothing but the image sought by investors greedy for profit. He has done that both as director of the IBA Berlin, which initiated many internationally remarked buildings as part of cautious urban renovation, and as the architect of such notable edifices as the "Kant Triangle" with which he provided exemplary demonstration of how his *compères* can fulfil their responsibilities with regard to urban planning even in the case of individual buildings.

Of course the curious shape of this site, its unsettled situation, and the architectural surroundings constituted a challenge for Kleihues. With two straight sides along the Kant- and the Fasanenstraße, and a slightly convex curve parallel to the city railway viaduct, this site makes particular demands with regard to the structure and proportions of the new building. The surroundings are urbane with a theatre and an administrative court, an art centre, the Berlin stock exchange, and the Paris Bar. The architect responded with a striking tower consisting of two superimposed quadratic cubes whose facades are very differently structured. Linked to the lower cube is a triangular low building whose long side follows the curving railway line. By setting back the facade to the Kantstraße the architect has created a space enclosed by the building on two sides, which is made for contemplating the richly-adorned facade of the Theater des Westens across the road. Kleihues calls himself a "poetic rationalist", and that concept vividly elucidates the huge 34 ton, 18 m. high, and 22 m. long "cockscomb" of riveted metal, which turns on top of the building once wind force 3 is reached.

Further Reading:
Thorsten Scheer and Andrea Mesecke (Ed.), *Das Kant-Dreieck. Gebäudemonographie*, Berlin 1995

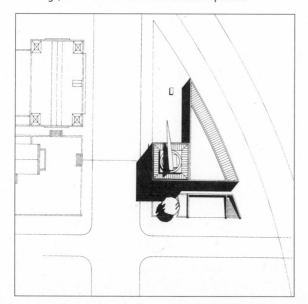

Architects: Hans Kollhoff and Helga Timmermann, Berlin
Building: Residential building
Location: Seesener Straße 70 a-f, Berlin-Wilmersdorf
Client: Onnasch Baubetreuung GmbH & Co, Berlin
Construction: 1992-1994

Hans Kollhoff
Helga Timmermann

● A visitor approaching this building from the Seesener Straße will be disappointed. From there only part of the back of the building can be seen through the entrance to the courtyard. The interesting south facade with the bend in the middle and the pleated steel and glass construction of the balconies faces the Stadtring, Germany's busiest motorway. That description makes clear why this site was long thought unus-

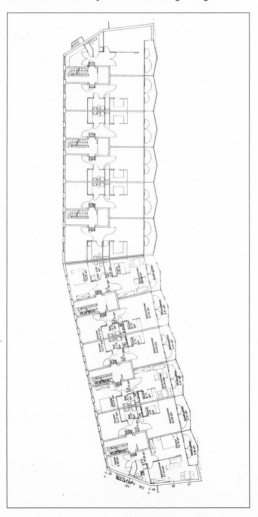

able. Nevertheless, it seemed architecturally desirable to create a new building to fill a gap between well-preserved and sometimes listed houses dating from the Gründerzeit, Jugendstil, and the thirties.
The architects solved the task of creating an attention-grabbing building for this gap in a way characteristic of Kollhoff. Instead of engaging in a dialogue with the adjoining houses, taking into consideration existing sightlines, window axes, and roofing, they chose confrontation, establishing the new building as a completely autonomous structure. However, despite all such demonstrative distancing, once again there is great closeness to the past. That is revealed in advocacy of solid architecture doing justice to the materials used, defending an ethos of craftsmanship even in the age of computer-aided design. The ground floor is thus clad in polished granite and other parts of the facade are in dark brick.
The 60 flats spread over six floors make a good impression with their parquet floors and tiled kitchens and bathrooms. Behind the balconies devised as sound-absorbent conservatories there are two-room flats with open kitchens and a room facing the quiet inner courtyard. On the two bottom floors 4-room maisonettes are available for young families. The attic storey dwellings, somewhat neglected in the facade, have open atrium-style landings.

Further Reading:
Falk Jaeger, *Wohnen am Verkehrsstrom*, in: VfA 5/1995, pp. 25-26

Architect: Peter Kulka, Cologne/Dresden
Building: Saxony's Parliament
Location: Holländische Straße, Dresden
Client: Freistaat Sachsen
Construction: 1991-1993

● After opening up of the Wall, bringing the GDR to an end, the federalism underpinning the former Federal Republic was extended to East Germany and five new Laender were established. Five new parliaments came into existence at the same time and had to be accomodated in more or less improvised fashion. Only Saxony decided to erect a new parliamentary building, which was planned and completed in record time. Normally only a very conventional building could have been produced in such circumstances, but Peter Kulka succeeded in devising an exceptionally impressive edifice – down to the constructional details – with a plenary chamber that seems to unite the idea of democracy with the practices of a "round table". The MPs sit in a complete circle, and that structure is reflected in the chamber's completely transparent curved facade. It is hardly conceivable that a modern parliament could be more "accessible" than the building in Dresden.

Peter Kulka's plan was inspired by Dresden's unique city skyline, shaped by the Brühlsche Terrace, the Residence and Hofkirche, the Zwinger, and the Semper Opera with low buildings fronting the Elbe and higher constructions with domes and towers further back.

The new parliament building confirms this structure by being prolonged in front of a five-storey late twenties building with a 36 m. high tower. MPs offices and parliamentary staff are accomodated in this older building which has been appropriately restored and renovated. The plenary chamber is extended by a long two-storey entrance area, containing a large foyer and admission to visitors galleries. Conceiving public access to the new building as the main entrance emphasizes the fact that a parliament open to its citizens has been built in Dresden.

Further Reading:
Bauten des Sächsischen Landtages in Dresden, in: CENTRUM Jahrbuch Architektur und Stadt 1994, pp. 84-91

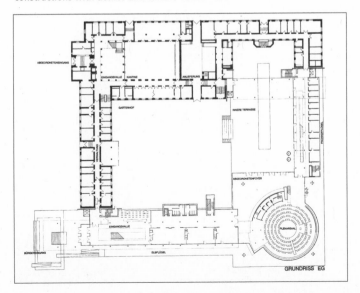

GRUNDRISS EG

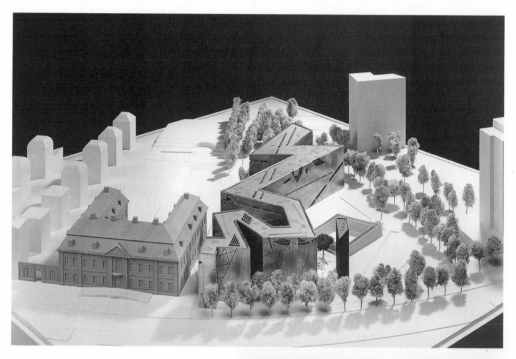

Architect: Daniel Libeskind, Berlin/Los Angeles
Building: Jewish Museum
Location: Lindenstraße, Berlin
Client: Land Berlin
Construction: 1993-1996

● The Jewish Museum is an extraordinary building in every respect. It makes little sense to merely consider the avantgarde aspect of a construction that cuts through the site like a flash of lightning. The overall concept of Libeskind's design absolutely merits being taken seriously.

Aspects critical of civilization are much more insistent than architectural considerations in plans which present "emptiness" as their central content. That refers to the vacuum created by the destruction of Jews and their cultural manifestation in Berlin and Germany. This museum is intended to make this loss directly felt rather than establishing documented distance. It therefore takes on the character of something fragmentary, something broken and incomplete, that wants to make architecturally manifest what is no longer visible. To that end the entire building is pervaded by a "spatial axis of emptiness". This is meant to entice the museum visitor out of his or her traditional status of observer, arousing scepticism about a culture that made the Holocaust possible.

The Jewish Museum is an extension of the Berlin Museum with which it is linked by a subterranean labyrinth. However, what one sees is anything but an extension in the usual sense. The new edifice's zig-zag form does not just seem to want to tear itself away from the old baroque building in a wild gesture. That also asserts an aesthetic autonomy, establishing irreconcilable conflict with any other architecture. Reconciliation could not be the theme for a museum that does not dispose over any artefacts but is instead a place of reflection on their destruction. That tragic state of affairs opened up an unusually large degree of freedom of action for the architect. He utilized it in such a way that this building cannot but be viewed as an artefact.

Further Reading:
Daniel Libeskind, *Jewish Museum,* Berlin 1992

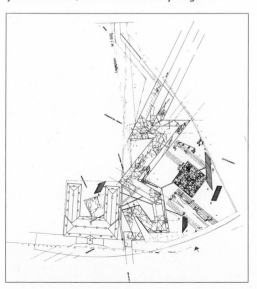

Architects: von Gerkan, Marg, and Partners
Planning: Volkwin Marg
Engineering: Polonyi & Partners, Cologne
Schlaich, Bergermann, & Partners, Stuttgart
Building: Trade Fair buildings
Location/Client: Leipzig/City of Leipzig
Construction: 1993-1996

● Many big inner city projects are close to completion and mighty efforts towards extensive but cautious urban renewal enjoy critical recognition, but a spectacular mega-project on the outskirts of Leipzig – the new trade fair site – has long eclipsed all other large-scale architectural developments. The fourth chapter in the history of trade fairs at Leipzig was implemented in the shortest possible time. The first step occurred in the Middle Ages, making the city into Germany's oldest centre for big trade fairs. The second got under way at the end of the 19th century when traditional mercantile gatherings were transformed into a model trade fair set-up. That resulted in the great commercial buildings which today still shape Leipzig's city centre. The third step occurred just a little later with the erection in 1913 of what is by now the "former trade fair site" along a central axis from the New City Hall to the monument to the Battle of the Nations. The new site in the north of the city breaks with a particular aspect of such facilities in Leipzig – integration in the inner city area. Time will tell whether that was a far-sighted decision.

Renovation of the former trade fair site whose most important buildings had been destroyed during the war only became a possibility after re-unification. However, the city authorities thought the estimated costs of between 700 and 800 million DM too high since renewal would also lead to demands for better links with the motorway and airport. For just under twice that sum the new trade fair site – with five halls (each 20,000 sq. m.), a congress centre, and an administration building – has come into being. All these edifices are parallel to the main axis containing the architectural highpoint, the central glass hall. This glass hall has justly attracted the attention of architectural critics – and not just because of its impressive size (250 m. long and 120 m. wide). It is above all the bold, apparently floating steel and glass construction that merits admiration, documenting as it does the skills of Germany's two most important structural engineers, Stefan Polonyi and Jörg Schlaich. External girders support and strengthen the narrow-mesh lattice construction to which the unframed glass is attached using "frogs feet". The outcome is incomparable transparency, endowing the glass hall with a generosity and openness to the world desirable for the trade fair site as a whole.

Further reading: Stefan W. Krieg, *Neue Messe Leipzig*, in: DAM Jahrbuch für Architektur 1996, pp. 80-84
Volkwin Marg (Ed.), *New Trade Fair Leipzig*, Birkhäuser Verlag, Basel 1996

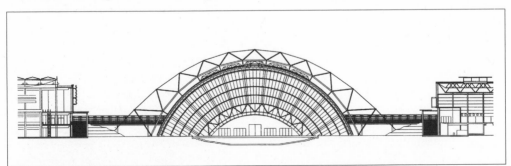

Architect: Richard Meier & Partners, New York
Building: Museum of Arts and Crafts
Location: Schaumainkai 17, Frankfurt a. M.
Client: Stadt Frankfurt am Main
Construction: 1982-1985

Richard Meier

99

● At the end of the seventies the Frankfurt city authorities devoted particular attention to the inner city and its representative buildings. At the centre of these endeavours to upgrade the city's image was development of what is known as the "museum bank", involving the south side of the river Main between the "Eiserne Steg" and the Friedensbrücke. The idea was that existing museums should be enlarged and new exhibition centres added during the course of the eighties. The plan was for a chain totalling eight buildings where the riverside site, wide shoreline promenade, and avenue of plane trees would create a unified urban experience. The city did in fact manage to implement its ambitious programme except for a new museum of musical instruments and extension of the museum of ethnology.

The 1979 competition for expanding the Museum of Arts and Crafts was tailor-made for New York architect Richard Meier in whose work twenties "white modernism" is resurrected. After all, in its new building ventures the city had given itself the task of following on from the great achievements of Ernst May and his comrades-in-arms after the first world war. Meier's building establishes an elegant bridge to that time and also impressively integrates the old Villa Metzler, built in 1803, which served after 1945 as an exhibition forum even though only a small part of the collection could be shown. Despite its size, the new building with 7,000 sq. m. of additional exhibition space has taken up the proportions of the old construction from which the architect derived a module to be found in the three parts of the new construction whose ground-plan constitutes a square together with the villa.

Meier's building of course profits from the beautiful little park between it and the museum of ethnology. It also benefits from the 30,000 objects in an internationally celebrated collection, consisting of top-quality manifestations of European and Asian arts and crafts. The architect has housed these in a highly structured landscape of display-cases, showing that in this building exhibits should be subordinate to his concepts of space.

Further Reading:
The Museum für Kunsthandwerk, in: A + U, September 1985, pp. 15-48

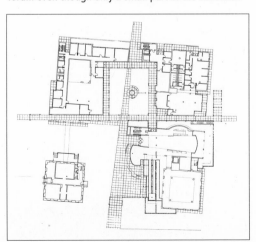

Architects: Carlfried Mutschler & Joachim Langner, Mannheim
Engineering: Frei Otto & Ewald Bubner, Warmbronn
Structural Engineering: Ove Arup & Partners, London
Building: Multi-Purpose Hall
Location: Herzogenriedpark, Mannheim
Client: Bundesgartenschau Mannheim GmbH
Construction: 1974-1975

● This multi-purpose hall, a building involving nothing but a roof, was called the "miracle of Mannheim" when it was constructed because no-one quite believed that an edifice consisting of shells made from wooden lattice-work would survive without supports. Despite all the calculations entailed this concept was in fact a courageous experiment since no guaranteed formal knowledge existed in this sphere. The unconventional structure was developed in pilot projects, which in principle functioned very similarly to Antoni Gaudí's old string models.

In such celebrated buildings as the Sagrada Familia church (1883-1926) in Barcelona, Gaudí attempted to develop "Gothic" architecture without buttresses. For that the pillars had to be installed diagonally. In order to become aware of the exact inclination and the overall constructional play of forces in his designs, he constructed models made from string on which he hung weights corresponding to the load individual pillars would have to support. The string lines demonstrated the precise structure of the vaulting, viewed upside down. Frei Otto proceeded similarly when he had the lattice-work multi-purpose hall structure, constructed from roof rafters, first made in thin wire so that he could see the play of forces and precise form taken by the vaulting. When the hall was assembled all the wooden slats were lightly screwed together on the ground in a grid of 50 by 50 cm, and then propped

in position by using scaffolding at exactly the height where the model had shown that they should be fixed until the entire roof was thus secure. After that the shell was spanned with light-permeable PVC-layered Trevira material.

The architects had hit on the hall's unusual form by incorporating the surroundings' hilly nature in construction of the building, wishing to create a spatially plastic "multi-purpose organism" that would be filled with flowers and floral activities for the half year duration of the Federal Garden Show and after that with all kinds of events: exhibitions, pop concerts, winter balls, sporting competitions, and circus presentations. The hope was thus to have created a focal-point for a new district in Mannheim.

Further Reading:
Die Multihalle auf der Bundesgartenschau, in: Baumeister 8/1975, pp. 702-711

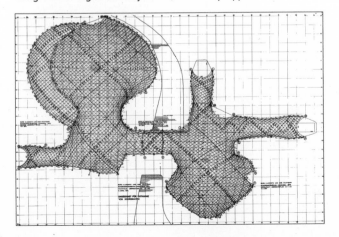

Architect: Gustav Peichl, Vienna
Building: Federal German Art and Exhibition Hall
Location: Friedrich-Ebert-Allee, Bonn
Client: Bundesbauministerium, Bonn
Construction: 1989-1992

● The new buildings housing the Bonn Art Museum and the Federal German Art and Exhibition Hall lie on the main road bissecting Bonn, within sight of the government quarter. From afar a welcome also emanates from the three light-towers, covered with blue tiles and pointing into the skies, that Gustav Peichl put on top of his building like funny hats – a building that mainly radiates dignity and pathos, and arouses an impression of monumentality.

The fortress-like mass of this urban gallery offers a number of surprises behind its walls. Immediately after passing through the narrow high doorway of the public entrance one enters a light-filled inner courtyard, adorned with a deciduous tree reflected in the wave-like glass facade of the foyer. Inside the building the interplay of enclosed cabinets and an open succession of rooms continues. A large exhibition hall is accompanied by a two-storey atrium, three smaller galleries, and a central cabinet. Out in the open a staircase leads up to the roof, covered with plants. In the place where ceiling windows are usually installed the architect has established a sculpture garden.

The building's central function is ongoing organization of several simultaneous and changing exhibitions, but a diverse programme of congresses, workshops, films, and musical events is also on offer. That is served by a 500-seat auditorium with the most modern conference technology, which can also be incorporated in the exhibition area. Siting the Federal Art Gallery near the Federal Chancellor's Office signifies that politics and culture aim at fulfilling a shared task in Germany. That involves all the federal Laender so the architect placed 16 dark metal pillars along the Friedrich-Ebert-Allee, intended to symbolize the 16 Laender as "pillars of German culture". The three light-towers on the roof represent the trinity of visual arts: architecture, painting, and sculpture.

Further Reading:
Dieter Bartetzko, *Kunst- und Austellungshalle der Bundesrepublik Deutschland,* Berlin 1992

Architects: Hans Scharoun with Edgar Wisniewski, Berlin
Building: Prussian State Library
Location: Potsdamer Straße, Berlin
Client: Stiftung Preußischer Kulturbesitz
Construction: 1969-1978

● The concept for the state library was produced at the same time as that for its prominent neighbour, Mies van der Rohe's Neue Nationalgalerie (1962-68), but an extended phase of planning and implementation resulted in this late work by Hans Scharoun, whose golden-oxidized aluminium book storage units adjoin Berlin's Cultural Forum to the east, belonging to a later age. As early as 1963 the Federal Building Directorate organized a restricted competition for construction of the state library and Scharoun emerged as the victor. The jury praised the architectural concept underlying a plan that took into account existing and planned buildings in the Culture Forum – both the proportions of the Philharmonie and the low Nationalgalerie (then at the planning stage) to which the hilly landscape of the library building gradually descended.

Scharoun died in 1972 during the four-year preparatory period. Planning was continued by his partner Edgar Wisniewski who had already worked on the inner structure of this large library during the competition phase. With this edifice and its many functional demands Scharoun had not been able to devise one of his "primary sketches" as the basis for all further planning. However, there is a guideline: the idea of unity of the sciences. The architects envisaged the library being used by an educated citizen strolling through the empire of books rather than by an expert in a hurry, looking neither to right or left as he seeks the quickest possible route to specialized literature. For this stroller a "reading room landscape" was developed: a diversely comprehensive space with a total length of 160 m., broken up into several levels with exciting views and niches, putting an emphasis on an individual working atmosphere for visitors to the library. A completely automated communication system with 64 reception-points was installed so as to allow borrowing books in as many places as possible.

Further Reading:
Ekkehart Vesper (Ed.): *Staatsbibliothek Preußischer Kulturbesitz,* Wiesbaden 1978

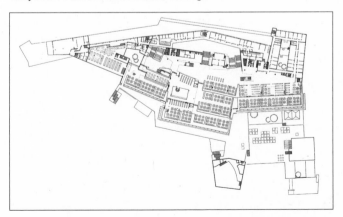

Architect: Karljosef Schattner, Eichstätt
Building: "Ulmer Hof"
Location: Pater-Philipp-Jenningen-Platz 6, Eichstätt
Client: Katholische Universität Eichstätt
Construction: 1978-1980

● The small Bavarian diocesan and university town of Eichstätt has become a centre for new buildings in old surroundings thanks to the activities of Karljosef Schattner, formerly the bishopric's architect. An instructive walk through the little town could easily be devised, leading past a considerable number of exemplary buildings demonstrating that an exciting dialogue can be set up between history and the present day. The architectural significance of Schattner's work only became apparent to Eichstätt's authorities and citizens as a result of mounting international interest. The town's particularly privileged position with many old buildings surviving wars and the passing of time meant that Schattner was mainly concerned with changes of use. His readiness to preserve historic substance and his ability to develop an individual modern formal language could thus be fully implemented. That was also the case with the Ulmer Hof, a venerable old building erected at the start of the 17th century and given its present form in 1688. People lived there until the 19th century, and then from 1842 a high school took over. In 1977 it was decided that the Catholic University's theology faculty and library should be moved into the by then empty building.

The Ulmer Hof was thus restored and rebuilt, and the inner courtyard was made into a modern library. What was formerly part of the exterior is transformed in such a way that a library user remains constantly aware that what is now inside was once outside. Today the building seems to be equally shaped by both historical and modern structural elements. In front of the former covered walk is a mighty construction of steel and glass, and the courtyard filled with desks is bordered to the south by the new book storage facilities, consisting of a perforated facade with metal gallery-balustrades. Above everything floats a light steel roof carried by fanned truss beams and separated from the old house walls by strips of ceiling-windows. Contrast and distance regulate the relationship between old and new in such a way that no-one would ever think that either could unfold better without the other.

Further Reading:
Umbau des Ulmer Hofes zu einer Fachbereichsbibliothek, in: Stahl und Form, Munich 1987, pp. 10-13

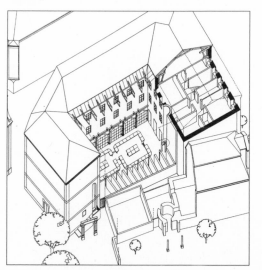

Architect: Karljosef Schattner, Eichstätt
Building: Diocesan Archive
Location: Luitpoltstraße 1, Eichstätt
Client: Bischöfliches Ordinariat Eichstätt
Construction: 1989-1992

● Karljosef Schattner has emphasized that his ideas were developed in response to the requirement that "transitions should not be blurred; yesterday and today should be clearly separated; and stratification should be shown". What is really remarkable about his work, however, is that unexpected spatial situations arise as a result of the highly contrasted interaction of historical and modern architectural elements. New buildings and conversions are always structured in such a way that they can stand as independent opposites but their spatial combination results in a new architectural quality. Schattner has demonstrated that in many buildings including the diocesan museum, the diocesan seminar, the student centre, the faculty of journalism, and the psychological institute. The latter conceals behind its unified modern north facade two 16th century buildings which have been combined as the institute. This principle of spatial layering is also apparent in the last building Schattner produced as diocesan architect. Restoration of the rather dilapidated baroque bishop's palace included making the building into a new administrative centre for the diocesan archive. An ugly extension dating from the fifties was pulled down and replaced by the new archive building. The elaborately structured facade with its long double window slits turns out on closer inspection to be a wall which the architect has imposed, like a second skin, in front of the concrete building containing the archive storage facilities. In terms of its inner organization this is a comparatively unspectacular building whose lower floors are used for storing old manuscripts from dissolved parish archives. Perhaps that was the reason why Schattner took particular care in structuring the exterior architecture. Alongside the facade, upgraded through the ornamentation of non-functional windows, it is mainly the projecting, floating, slice-like roof – whose blood-red underside contrasts powerfully with the white plastered wall – that attracts attention. However, the glass stairwell, linking the old and new buildings, also merits consideration. Reflected in its dark glass is the historical facade whose windows seem to grow out of the modern archive building.

Further Reading:
Das Diözesanarchiv in Eichstätt, in: DAM Jahrbuch für Architektur 1994, pp. 142-145

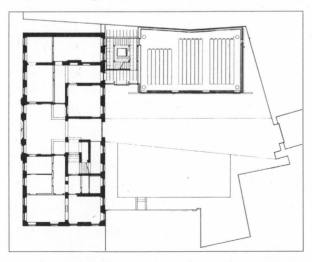

Architect: Axel Schultes, Berlin
Building: Bonn Art Museum
Location: Friedrich-Ebert-Allee 2, Bonn
Client: Stadt Bonn
Construction: 1988-1992

● At the beginning of 1985 Axel Schultes' design for the Bangert, Jansen, Scholz, and Schultes partnership won the competition for ideas for Bonn's art museum and the federal art gallery. This involved two 300 m. long walls parallel to the road, providing protection allowing the two museums to open up to one another. However, at the end of 1985 a separate competion was held for the federal gallery and that was won by Gustav Peichl, the Viennese architect. His hermetic monument, shutting itself off from both the city of Bonn and its art museum, obeys rules that clearly contradict Schultes' concept.

In order to save the original idea of inner transparency in construction of the art museum the abandoned protective function of the long outer walls had to be made good by another architectural element. Schultes, who had by then separated from his former partners, found that in the idea of a "large roof". Such a roof was intended to replace the wall as the spatial edge of the new museum building. At the same time it had to satisfy the planner's ambition of creating a building full of vital daylight. The architect spoke of "light falling through the coffered roof into the rooms below like water through a sieve", flooding all the walls and corridors.

Schultes' museum has a square ground-plan and access is gained diagonally. The idea of shielding the exhibition area from the road was not abandoned. The administrative rooms, grouped in a frontal tract, take on the function of a protective wall. The great roof extends over all parts of the building, providing outstanding light. In no other museum are the paintings of August Macke and the Rhenish Expressionists, and works by such artists as Beuys, Polke, Palermo, Richter, Baselitz, and Kiefer so well presented. It is not just chance that an architect who makes the experience of space into a professional obsession has succeeded in creating a building *for* art rather than one that overwhelms modern paintings, objects, and sculpture through its own aesthetic pretensions.

Further Reading:
Axel Schultes, *Kunstmuseum Bonn,* ed. Charlotte Frank, Berlin 1994

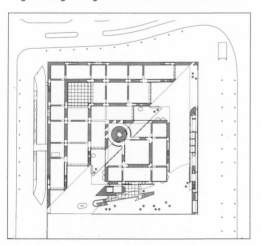

Architects: Peter C. von Seidlein, H. Fischer, C. Winkler,
E. Effinger, Munich
Building: Newspaper Printing Works
Location: Zamdorfer Straße, Munich-Steinhausen
Client: Süddeutscher Verlag, Munich
Construction: 1983-1984

● The Süddeutsche Zeitung first appeared in October 1945, produced at a half-destroyed printing works in the centre of Munich. Lack of paper meant that it could only appear three times a week to start with, but as time passed this became Germany's most-bought daily newspaper. That success made increasing demands of restricted space at the established printing works, so the company moved to the Steinhausen district of Munich. Steinhausen is a typical industrial area, characterized by a complete lack of architectural merit until the Peter C. Steidlein combine demonstrated that industrial building could produce fascinating results.

The task facing an architect designing industrial buildings involves allowing the production process to manifest as clearly as possible. Instead of jamming a uniform box onto a firm with a multi-level production process, what must be done is to reflect specific activities in a differentiated structure. The architects of this printing works thus devised a huge multiply-structured area, consisting of four successive extended components. In the south paper is delivered by road and rail, so it is stored there. That is followed by the rotation hall with house-high printing machinery. The two areas form a uniform four-storey building. In front of it, to the north, is a two-storey hall for further processing and deliveries. As a connecting link there are seven stairwell towers and between them sloping glazing through which the rotation hall is provided with daylight and differences in height are compensated for. A steel construction of pillars and open girders, fixed to the concrete stairwell towers, spans the two halls.

This building, extending along an east-west axis for as much as 180 m., is easy to comprehend with its stepped form and the accentuation provided by the towers. The filigrane structuring on which the construction is based endows the printing works with transparency, making the building shine from within during the early evening. Throughout the day the silver of its aluminium panelling glitters. Inside illumination from the north endows the entire hall with a floating lightness.

Further Reading:
Peter C. von Seidlein, *Zeitungsdruckerei Süddeutscher Verlag,* in:
Bauen mit Stahl No. 67, pp. 35-37

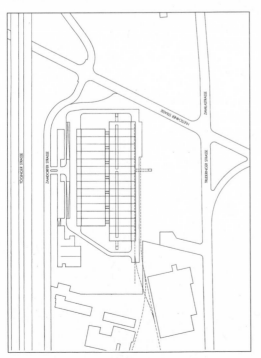

Architects: Alvaro Siza, Porto, with Peter Brinkert, Berlin
Building: "Bonjour Tristesse" Flats
Location: Schlesische Straße 7, Berlin-Kreuzberg
Client: Harald Schulz, Berlin
Construction: 1982-1984

● One fine day the title of Françoise Sagan's celebrated novel was unmissably blazoned on Alvaro Siza's building as if it had been branded on a forehead. Bonjour Tristesse – with a reversed s – wrote the outraged sprayer, thereby absolutely capturing the architect's intentions. Since that time Siza has in fact used this name for the house he devised for the IBA Berlin. The provocative inscription is virtually the only adornment of a building whose austere charm seems to be a cry of protest – against post-modern architecture and its striving for harmony, against a tendency towards trivialization and forced irony.

"Bonjour Tristesse" is a block of flats with some shops on the ground floor, which hides behind a provocatively monotonous facade with regularly-placed window-holes. The annoyance of many passers-by with this monstrosity seems all too justified. However, viewed as whole, this building is an ornament, a sculptural demonstration. The architect has shaped his building like a gigantic piece of rubber which can be bent as required. That is most clearly apparent in the inner courtyard. There Alvaro Siza has constructed a crease without precedent in the history of building. Yet one must ask this man, who made a name for himself in publicly-subsidized housing after the Portuguese revolution of 1974, to what extent he thought of the inhabitants when devising this edifice.

The building's curvaceous forms seem to have inspired the architect to develop highly unconventional divisions within the ground-plan. The monotonous placing of the windows – behind which might be repetitive hotel rooms – in fact contrasts very greatly with the spatial diversity they conceal. In the inner courtyard there are unglazed windows set in front of pergolas, and the windows facing the road open onto little conservatory-like protective zones. The flats themselves demonstrate experimental delight in division of space in both the apartments and the four-room dwellings. A complex living structure of accomodation and access areas is hidden within a building whose outer appearance is so uncompromisingly regimented.

Further Reading:
Apartment Building in Kreuzberg, in: Abitare 226/1984, pp. 56-59

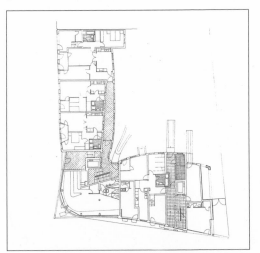

Architects: Otto Steidle + Partners, Munich
Uwe Kiessler + Partners, Munich
Implementation: Peter Schweger + Partners, Hamburg
Building: Press Centre
Location: Underground station Baumwall, Hamburg
Client: Gruner & Jahr
Construction: 1987-1990

● The new press centre on the Elbe promenade constitutes an autonomous quarter in Hamburg, providing employment for 2,500. This is bisected by a public path linking the harbour with the "Hamburger Michel". Along the east side of the editorial building, facing the Elbe, a footbridge leads to the centre of this creation. A little square is dominated by a round tower which marks the main entrance and entices passersby into a terrace café. Cultivation of contacts between the people who work here and the local population was one of the guidelines underlying a construction intended to make an impact on this district. An open "media town" with small alleys and courtyard-like street areas was thus devised rather than a unified administrative complex.

In order to develop a small-scale, adaptable building the architects chose a dual structure (a long hallway flanked by offices to the right and left) with access areas lit from above. The offices, hallways, and stairwells all benefit from daylight. Ventilation of the offices, situated behind planted courtyards and balconies, takes place through the windows. The architects have thus achieved their overall objective of creating a working world with residential qualities.

In shaping the outer facades the architects were guided by associations arising from the harbour and its characteristic buildings. However, more important than direct allusions, as expressed in the riverside portholes and the balcony railings, was adoption of the historical siting of former warehouses in this old harbour city. That presented itself as a solution because, on the one hand, it permitted architectural integration of the gigantic press centre in this quarter and, on the other, it made possible highly flexible utilization.

Overall the intention was to establish "an architecture of simple means" as demonstrated in the painted wooden window-frames in the upper storeys. Nevertheless the aggressive sea air made it necessary to clad all the structural elements with crafted titanium sheet-zinc.

Further Reading:
Pressehaus Gruner & Jahr, in: DAM Jahrbuch für Architektur 1991, pp. 82-99

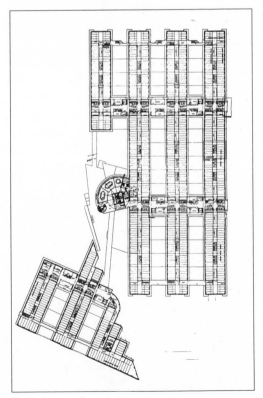

Architects: Otto Steidle + Partners, Munich
Colour Concept: Erich Wiesner, Berlin
Building: West University
Location: "Oberer Eselsberg", Ulm
Client: Finanzministerium Baden-Württemberg
Construction: 1990-1994

● Modern architecture has for the most part only accepted diversity of colour in contrasting materials and reflections of light. Only with the rehabilitation of historical buildings has the use of colour been honoured once again but without any great enthusiasm. In our part of the world there only seems to be consensus about using colour on such structurally employed materials as steel and wood. In fact in recent years wood has enjoyed a real revival as a building material, frequently in the form of large-scale cladding for facades. Otto Steidle has played a considerable part in that. It was thus just a matter of time before painted facades exerted a powerful impact on his designs.

A group of radiantly coloured buildings has been produced for the new faculty of engineering created as part of expansion of Ulm university. The extended

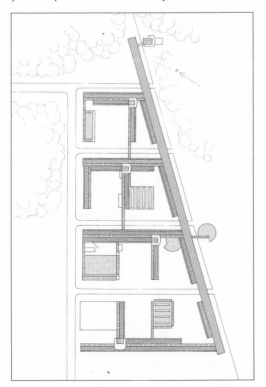

wooden facades are resplendent in pale green, yellow, orange, a powerful blue, and even "Italian pink". Such an abundance of colour-contrasts is unusual in Germany. However, Otto Steidle wished to design a building that was unconventional in several respects, providing excitingly restless surroundings for creative research. Art and science come close in the demand for creativity. The architect sought that closeness in "science city Ulm", which wants to be a model of future-oriented research. He accorded with that desire in creating a lively ensemble of much-used teaching areas and hermetic research facilities.

The "Universität West" is devised as a site with four low "quarters", linked to the south by a 300 m. long wooden building on stilts. The latter contains lecture halls and seminar rooms while the institute buildings and workshops are in the "quarters". The two lecture hall buildings, one blue and one yellow, are circular in accordance with their use as places of assembly. Where the internal communication systems cross stand the four quarter towers in whose upper floors meeting-rooms and libraries are to be found. A fifth tower, marking the far end of the access-line in a powerful red, houses the cafeteria and faculty rooms. All these buildings have been given a wooden facade, and only the lower tower floors reveal that they are constructed of reinforced concrete.

Further Reading:
Universität West in Ulm, in: CENTRUM Jahrbuch Architektur und Stadt 1994, pp. 124-129

Architects: James Stirling, Michael Wilford, & Ass., London
Building: Neue Staatsgalerie
Location: Konrad-Adenauer-Straße, Stuttgart
Client: Land Baden-Württemberg
Construction: 1977-1984

● No other building of the eighties sparked off such architectural controversy as Stirling's Staatsgalerie. Even today this building, which also includes a small theatre, seems uniquely strange amid the German architectural landscape. Nevertheless people have calmed down and critical spirits have long made peace with this colourful collage consisting of elements of ancient Egyptian, Classical, and disrespectful Pop culture. The reason for that is not just a matter of having got used to the building. The fact is that this inventively theatrical architecture houses rooms which serve effective presentation of the museum's splendid collection of paintings.

The upper floor in particular, the actual gallery, groups the exhibition rooms, all with light from above, in the tradional U-form which eliminates problems with orientation. The architecture remains neutral and does not distract the public from contemplation of art.

There is a succession of agreeably proportioned rooms with white walls and parquet floors, differing only in size. The exaggeratedly large numbers on the gable-adorned doorways between rooms demonstrate both where one is and also that the architect was possessed by mischief wherever he showed off his skills. The museum that Stirling built next to the old Staatsgalerie comments ironically on its own premisses. Confronted by the traffic speeding past on an eight-lane main road and the sloping site, it seemed reasonable to devise a fortress-like edifice. So the architect resorted to all the possible stylistic characteristics he thought appropriate here without, however, striving for an authoritative monument. In order to prevent that he subverted the solemnity of a building clad in natural sandstone and travertine with pipelines painted lilac-pink and baby-blue, serving as larger-than-life railings. In the rotunda courtyard he draped an ancient Egyptian cemetery gate with scantily clad beauties made of white marble. The Neue Staatsgalerie thus became an architecture of humorous experiences, and it is only logical that a public path should go right through it. It demonstrates to interested passers-by a concept that has in the meantime attracted followers: dissolution of a unified architectural complex into an exciting setting, broken up by courtyards, staircases, and alleys.

Further Reading:
Christoph Hackelsberger, *Neue Staatsgalerie Stuttgart,* in: Der Architekt 7-8/1984, pp. 343-348

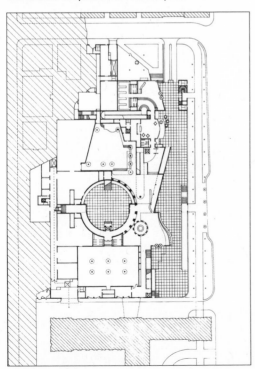

Architects: James Stirling, Michael Wilford, & Ass., London
with Walter Nägeli, Berlin
Building: Company development
Location: Pfieffewiesen, near Melsungen
Client: B. Braun Melsungen AG
Construction: 1986-1992

● South of Kassel the task was to adapt extensive company development to a rolling hilly landscape. The architects thus devised landscape-related elements with which the entire site was structured. Across the valley they situated a long access tract, linking the administration building and the production area parallel to the valley axis. Access and production thus divide the company area into two halves: the eastern zone devised as a park intended to create a transition between nature and architecture, and the western area with rows of warehouses and transportation facilities. The latter and the square in front constitute a striking conclusion to this site. The administrative building is the architectural highpoint whose most remarkable characteristic involves the upturned cone-shaped supports which seem to balance rather than carry the edifice's three floors. To the long concrete access wall, leading from here into the works area, a wooden bridge is attached, providing pedestrian access to almost all the halls. At the heart of the site is the centre for the distribution of goods, constructed as a succession of spaces where individual functions – incoming goods, checking, storage, packing, etc – receive differentiated expression. The elliptically shaped goods distribution facilities with a diagonally downwards sloping pre-patinaed copper roof immediately attracts attention. Stirling wanted ageing processes to be reflected in the buildings.

For the architecture of the production building, where medical products made of synthetic materials are manufactured, the main intention was to situate the areas where most people worked in the upper storeys. Analysis of the production sequence did in fact show that vertical organization would be advantageous. Labour-intensive work-spheres could thus be elevated sufficiently high above other buildings to permit extensive views into the landscape. 12 m. high concrete pillars support the platform containing the production areas. Above that is a barrel roof spanning 30 m.

Further Reading:
Vielfalt. Die Fabrik B. Braun Melsungen AG, in: db deutsche bauzeitung 1/1993, pp. 14-26

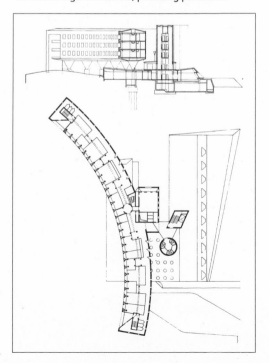

Architect: Zvonko Turkali, Frankfurt a. M.
Building: Civic Centre
Location: Mühlstraße, Guntersblum
Client: Ortsgemeinde Guntersblum
Construction: 1993-1995

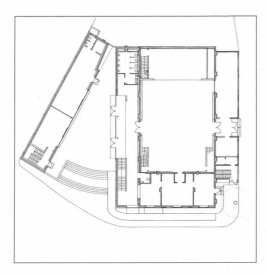

● Opposite a favourite destination for excursions, where a former branch of the Rhine circumscribes a beautiful nature reserve, lies the Palatinate community of Guntersblum with its half-timbered houses and farm buildings in undressed stone. Here a gym dating from 1929 was to be modernized, and a foyer, several multi-purpose rooms for local clubs, and a library added. Zvonko Turkali, the Yugoslav-born architect, has now augmented the old gym with a narrow foyer construction along the entire length of the western side and positioned an equally slender new building, containing club rooms and a library, at an angle to the main block. The two tracts diverge like scissors so that the small street ("An der Kleier") is at last appropriately completed and a little space created between the buildings.

The two-storey foyer and the new library building are both reinforced concrete skeletal constructions faced with the undressed stone characteristic of Guntersblum. Their modern cube-like character is emphasized – rather than relativized – by the contrast with the striking stonework, which creates an obvious link with the town buildings. The recent addition has a desk-roof sloping towards the road, and a line of high windows facing the courtyard providing light for the upper-storey library. Concentrated utilization is thus possible without renunciation of daylight.

Further Reading:
Bürgerhaus Guntersblum, in: Bauwelt 9/1996, pp. 456-458

Architect: Oswald Mathias Ungers, Cologne
Building: Baden Land Library
Location: Erbprinzenstraße, Karlsruhe
Client: Land Baden-Württemberg
Construction: 1979-1984

● To relieve a drastic lack of space at the Baden Land Library it was decided in the seventies that a new building should be erected on a site opposite the classical Stephanskirche. Oswald Mathias Ungers won the competition held in 1979 with a proposal to put up buildings along the Herrenstraße and the Ritterstraße. The existing buildings and trees on the site were largely to be preserved and integrated in the new plan. The overall area consists of three elements: the small-scale, architecturally unified houses on the Herrengasse; a middle zone with trees, bounded by a house in the classical style and a new gate-building on the Erbprinzenstraße; and the geometrically austere block of the new library enclosing an inner courtyard.

In his structuring of the modern edifice the architect took into account the existing buildings and Friedrich Weinbrenner's Stephanskirche whose porch is reflected in the library's gabling. Ungers also picked up other aspects of the church – its original dome and the square ground-plan. In his design the measurements and siting of the different parts of the building (inclu-

sive of paving stones and tiles) follow a structural order derived from the square. Over the reading room is a dome adorned with historicizing coffering in plaster – behind which the real construction of curved lime-wood beams is hidden.

The body of the library consist of a core and a lower ring, surrounding the inner elements like a shell. The latter takes up the scale of existing buildings in the Ritterstraße while the "core" – out of which the "shell" seems to grow – responds to the gable-level of the Stephanskirche. The materials employed accorded with that concept. The shell is rough, its walls are of stone, and the roof is covered with slates. The materials and colours employed in the core are more delicate. It is plastered and protected by a copper roof that creates an additional link with the Stephanskirche. The core and the shell are separated from one another by a glassed-over tract. Inside spheres of utilization are separated too. The shell thus mainly houses such internal functions as administration while reading rooms and book storage are in the core.

Further Reading:
Badische Landesbibliothek Karlsruhe, in: O. M. Ungers, Architektur 1951-1990, Stuttgart 1991, pp. 118-129

Architect: Oswald Mathias Ungers, Cologne
Building: Alfred Wegener Institute of Polar Research
Location: Columbusstraße, Bremerhaven
Client: Freie Hansestadt Bremen
Construction: 1980-1984

● The polar research institute at Bremerhaven seems to be anchored like a huge ocean liner from the heyday of such vessels. Above the dark high rump rises the radiant white deck construction with staircases, gangways, railings, and three huge round funnels. The architect's symbolic language could hardly be clearer, manifestly combining two traditions in his building: the steamer motif which threads through the history of modern architecture, and the brick constructions of the North German coastal region, cited in the polar research institute's clinker walls.

The combination of steamer motif and brick architecture was suggested by the site right next to the old harbour. The harbour basin and the Weser estuary circumscribe the historical urban area. The old structure of housing blocks still determines Bremerhaven's outer appearance. In his plan Ungers thus decided in favour of re-establishing and adding to that traditional structure within the urban ground-plan. That decision and a site offering extensive views of the Geeste estuary and the North Sea gave rise to a building which is both elegant and weighty.

Its massiveness results from the demands made of it. Four extensive functions had to be almost equally satisfied: laboratories and research facilities for geologists and marine biologists; social rooms inclusive of library and lecture hall; areas for storage, workshops, and logistics; and technical operations. A large part of the operational areas are lit artificially so they could be located at the heart of the building, allowing maximum utilization of the site in depth. Difficulties with the foundations necessitated abandonment of cellars so that storage and technical facilities had to be at ground-level. The advantage there is that the main functions are in upper floors, high above traffic on the six-lane Columbusstraße.

Further Reading:
Alfred-Wegener-Institut für Polarforschung, in: O. M. Ungers, Architektur 1951-1990, Stuttgart 1991, pp. 130-139

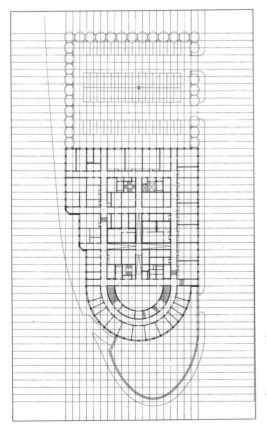

● Professional Associations

Bundesarchitektenkammer
Königswinterer Str. 709
D-53227 Bonn

Bund Deutscher Architekten (BDA)
Ippendorfer Allee 14 b
D-53127 Bonn

Bund Deutscher Baumeister (BDB)
Kennedyalle 11
D-53113 Bonn

Deutscher Werkbund e.V. (DWB)
Braubachstr. 33 A
D-60311 Frankfurt a. M.

Verband Deutscher Architekten- und
Ingenieurvereine (DAI)
Adenauerallee 58
D-53113 Bonn

● Archives and Collections

Aedes-Galerie und Architekturforum
Stadt-Bahnbogen 600
D-10623 Berlin

Architekturmuseum der
Technischen Universität München
Arcisstr. 21
D-80333 München

Bauhaus Archiv
Klingelhöferstr. 14
D-10785 Berlin

Deutsches Architektur-Museum
Schaumainkai 43
D-60596 Frankfurt a. M.

Hamburgisches Architekturarchiv
Bramfelder Str. 138
D-22305 Hamburg

Technische Universität Berlin
Plansammlung
Dovestr. 1–5
D-10587 Berlin

Werkbund Archiv
Martin-Gropius-Bau
Stresemannstr. 110
D-10963 Berlin

● Bibliography

1. Lexica

Contemporary European Architects (4 Vols.), Benedikt Taschen Verlag, Cologne 1994–96

Emanuel, Muriel (Ed.): *Contemporary Architects,* Gale Research International Ltd., Detroit 1994

Kadatz, Hans-Joachim (Ed.): *Seemanns Lexikon der Architektur,* Seemann Verlag, Zürich 1994

Lampugnani, Vittorio Magnago (Ed.): *Hatje-Lexikon der Architektur des 20. Jahrhunderts,* Verlag Gerd Hatje, Stuttgart 1983

Pevsner, Nikolaus/Honour, Hugh/Fleming, John (Ed.): *The Penguin Dictionary of Architecture,* Penguin Books, Harmondsworth 1991

2. Architecture in Germany

Architektur in der DDR, Schriften des Instituts für Städtebau und Architektur, Henschel-Verlag, Berlin 1980

Bauen heute. Architektur der Gegenwart in der Bundesrepublik Deutschland, exhibition catalogue by the German Architecture Museum, Ernst Klett Verlag, Stuttgart 1985

Bofinger, Helge and Margret, et. al.: *Architektur in Deutschland, Bundesrepublik und Westberlin,* Verlag W. Kohlhammer, Stuttgart 1981

Düwel, Jörn: *Baukunst voran! Architektur und Städtebau in der SBZ/DDR,* Berlin 1995

Feldmeyer, Gerhard G.: *Die neue deutsche Architektur,* with introduction by Manfred Sack, Verlag W. Kohlhammer, Stuttgart 1993

Jaeger, Falk: *Bauen in Deutschland. Ein Führer durch die Architektur des 20. Jahrhunderts in der Bundes-republik und in West-Berlin,* Verlag Gerd Hatje, Stuttgart 1985

Joedicke, Jürgen (Ed.): *Architektur in Deutschland '93. Deutscher Architekturpreis 1993,* Karl Krämer Verlag, Stuttgart 1994 *(The most important new buildings in Germany are presented bi-annually in this series)*

Krenz, Gerhard: *Architektur zwischen gestern und morgen,* Deutsche Verlags-Anstalt, Stuttgart 1975 *(Building in the GDR)*

Nerdinger, Winfried and Tafel, Cornelius: *Architectural Guide Germany – 20 th Century,* Birkhäuser Verlag, Basel 1996

Pehnt, Wolfgang: *German Architecture 1960–1970,* (English & German) Verlag Gerd Hatje, Stuttgart 1970

Zukowsky, John (Ed.): *Architektur in Deutschland 1919–1939,* Prestel Verlag, Munich 1994

3. Yearbooks

Jahrbuch für Architektur, ed. Deutsches Architektur-Museum, published 1980–1991 by Verlag Vieweg, Braunschweig and Wiesbaden

DAM Architektur Jahrbuch/Architecture Annual, ed. Deutsches Architektur-Museum, published since 1992 by Prestel-Verlag, Munich

Centrum. Jahrbuch für Architektur und Stadt, ed. Peter Neitzke & Carl Steckeweh, published since 1992 by Verlag Vieweg, Braunschweig and Wiesbaden

Jahrbuch Architektur in Hamburg, ed. Hamburgische Architektenkammer, published since 1989 by Junius Verlag Hamburg

Jahrbuch Architektur in Berlin, ed. Architektenkammer Berlin, published since 1992 by Junius Verlag Hamburg

4. Architectural Guides to Individual Cities

Architekturführer Berlin , Martin Wörner & Doris Mollenschott, with introduction by Wolfgang Schäche, Dietrich Reimer Verlag, Berlin 1994

Architekturführer Cottbus: Stadt und Umgebung, ed. Institut für Regionalentwicklung u. Strukturplanung, Verlag für Bauwesen, Berlin 1993

Architekturführer Frankfurt am Main, Bernd Kalusche & Wolf-Christian Setzepfandt, (German/English), Dietrich Reimer Verlag, Berlin 1992

Architekturführer Hamburg, Ralf Lange, Fellbach 1995

Architekturführer München, Katharina Bloh et al., with introduction by Winfried Nerdinger, (German/English), Dietrich Reimer Verlag, Berlin 1994

Berlin, Brandenburg. Ein Architekturführer, ed. IRS with Architekten- und Ingenieurverein zu Berlin (German/English), 2nd rev. edition, Ernst & Sohn Verlag, Berlin 1993

Architekturführer Köln: Profane Architektur nach 1900 by Helmuth Fußbroich, Verlag Bachem, Cologne 1997

Stuttgart. Ein Architekturführer, Martin Wörner & Gilbert Lupfer, with introduction by Frank R. Werner, Dietrich Reimer Verlag, Berlin 1997

5. Monographs

Alvar Aalto, Karl Fleig (German/French), 4th edition, Birkhäuser Verlag, Basel 1991

Tadao Ando, Masao Furuyama (German/English), 3rd enl. & updated edition, Birkhäuser Verlag, Basel 1996

Auer + Weber. Positionen und Projekte, ed. Klaus-Dieter Weiß, Edition baumeister, Munich 1993

Behnisch & Partner. Bauten 1952–1992, ed. Johann-Karl Schmidt & Ursula Zeller, Galerie der Stadt Stuttgart, Verlag Gerd Hatje, Stuttgart 1992

Heinz Bienefeld. Bauten und Projekte, ed. Manfred Speidel & Sebastian Legge, Verlag Walther König, Cologne 1991

Gottfried Böhm. Vorträge, Bauten, Projekte, ed. Svetlozar Raèv, Karl Krämer Verlag, Stuttgart/Zürich 1988

Egon Eiermann 1904–1970. Bauten und Projekte, ed. Wulf Schirmer, Deutsche Verlags-Anstalt, Stuttgart 1993

Norman Foster. Buildings and Projects , Volume 1–4, ed. Ian Lambot, Birkhäuser Verlag, Basel 1991–93

Frank Gehry und seine Architektur . Introduction by Henry N. Cobb, Wiese Verlag, Basel 1989

von Gerkan, Marg und Partner, Architektur 1991–1995, Meinhard von Gerkan (German/English), Birkhäuser Verlag, Basel 1996

Nicholas Grimshaw & Partner. Bauten u. Projekte, Colin Amery, Verlag Ernst & Sohn, Berlin 1996

Herman Hertzberger. Bauten und Projekte 1959–1986, Arnulf Lüchinger, Arch-Edition, Den Haag 1987

Thomas Herzog. Bauten 1978–1992, Verlag Gerd Hatje, Stuttgart 1993

Herzog & de Meuron: The Complete Works. Volume 2: 1989–1991, Gerhard Mack, (English/German) Birkhäuser Verlag, Basel 1996

Josef Paul Kleihues. ed. Andreas Mesecke & Thorsten Scheer, with introduction by Winfried Nerdinger (German/English), Birkhäuser Verlag, Basel 1996

Daniel Libeskind. Radix-Matrix. Architekturen und Schriften, ed. Alois M. Müller, Prestel, Munich/New York 1994

Richard Meier. Details, Werner Blaser
(German/English), Birkhäuser Verlag, Basel 1996

*Gustav Peichl. Neue Projekte, Gustav Peichl, Recent
Projects,* Walter Zschokke (German/English),
Birkhäuser Verlag, Basel 1996

Hans Scharoun. Die Forderung des Unvollendeten, ed.
Jörg C. Kirschenmann & Eberhard Syring, Deutsche
Verlags-Anstalt, Stuttgart 1993

Karljosef Schattner. Ein Architekt aus Eichstätt, ed.
Wolfgang Pehnt, Verlag Gerd Hatje, Stuttgart 1988

Axel Schultes, Projekte 1985–1991, ed. Charlotte
Frank (Edition Axel Meyer), Verlag Ernst & Sohn, Berlin
1992

Alvaro Siza, Peter Testa, Birkhäuser Verlag, Basel 1996

Otto Steidle. Werkmonographie, ed. Ulrich Conrads &
Manfred Sack, Verlag Vieweg, Braunschweig and Wiesbaden 1985

*James Stirling, Michael Wilford and Associates.
Buildings & Projects 1975–1992,* Verlag Gerd Hatje,
Stuttgart 1994

Oswald Mathias Ungers. Architektur 1951–1990,
Deutsche Verlags-Anstalt, Stuttgart 1991

6. Architectural Magazines

ARCH+
Zeitschrift für Architektur, Städtebau, Design
Published quarterly in Aachen

Baukultur
Technik, Wissenschaft, Kunst, Umwelt
Zeitschrift des Verbandes Deutscher Architekten- und
Ingenieurvereine (DAI)
Published bi-monthly in Wiesbaden

Baumeister
Zeitschrift für Architektur
Published monthly in Munich

Bauwelt
Published weekly in Berlin

Bauen in Beton
Published annually. Editor: Klaus Kinold, Munich

Daidalos
Architektur, Kunst, Kultur
Published quarterly in Berlin

Der Architekt
Zeitschrift des Bundes Deutscher Architekten (BDA)
Published monthly in Bonn

db deutsche bauzeitung
Zeitschrift des Bundes Deutscher Baumeister,
Architekten und Ingenieure (BDB)
Published monthly in Stuttgart

DBZ Deutsche Bauzeitschrift
Published monthly in Gütersloh

Detail
Zeitschrift für Architektur und Baudetail
Published eight times a year in Munich

Leonardo
Magazin für Architektur
Published every six weeks in Augsburg

● **Register**

● **Authors**

Gerd de Bruyn, b. 1954, Dr. phil., 1989-92 editor of "Baukultur", lives and works in Frankfurt am Main as a writer on architecture and city development.

Gerd Zimmermann, b. 1946, Dr. Eng., has been Professor of Planning and Architectural Theory since 1992. He is Rector of the Weimar Bauhaus University.

Wilfried Wang, b. 1957, is an architect, has been Professor for Planning and the History of Architecture at the Harvard University Graduate School of Design since 1996, and is director of the German Architecture Museum at Frankfurt am Main.